EUROPE/AMERICA

3

THIRD WORLD INSTABILITY
CENTRAL AMERICA
AS A EUROPEAN-AMERICAN ISSUE

EUROPE/AMERICA
3

THIRD WORLD INSTABILITY
CENTRAL AMERICA
AS A EUROPEAN-AMERICAN ISSUE

Andrew J. Pierre, Editor

Fernando Morán
Irving Kristol
Michael D. Barnes
Alois Mertes
Daniel Oduber

A Council on Foreign Relations Book
Published by
New York University Press
New York and London
1985

COUNCIL ON FOREIGN RELATIONS BOOKS

The Council on Foreign Relations, Inc., is a nonprofit and nonpartisan organization devoted to promoting improved understanding of international affairs through the free exchange of ideas. The Council does not take any position on questions of foreign policy and has no affiliation with, and receives no funding from, the United States government.

From time to time, books and monographs written by members of the Council's research staff or visiting fellows, or commissioned by the Council, or written by an independent author with critical review contributed by a Council study or working group are published with the designation "Council on Foreign Relations Book." Any book or monograph bearing that designation is, in the judgment of the Committee on Studies of the Council's board of directors, a responsible treatment of a significant international topic worthy of presentation to the public. All statements of fact and expressions of opinion contained in Council books are, however, the sole responsibility of the author.

First published in hard cover by New York University Press,
Washington Square, New York, N.Y. 10003

Library of Congress Cataloging in Publication Data
Main Entry under title:

Third World instability.

(Europe/America ; 3)
Includes bibliographical references.
1. Central America — Foreign relations — 1979–
Addresses, essays, lectures. 2. Central America — Foreign
relations — Europe — Addresses, essays, lectures.
3. Europe — Foreign relations — Central America — Addresses,
essays, lectures. 4. Central America — Foreign relations —
United States — Addresses, essays, lectures. 5. United
States — Foreign relations — Central America — Addresses,
essays, lectures.   I. Pierre, Andrew J.
II. Morán, Fernando, 1926–   .   III. Council on
Foreign Relations.   IV. Series.
F1439.5.T48   1985   327.728   85-4198
ISBN 0-8147-6594-7 (cloth)

The Project on
European-American Relations

Relations between Western Europe and the United States have become more turbulent in recent years. Divergences in interests and perceptions have grown. Many are questioning the fundamental assumptions of the postwar period. There is a broad consensus that the European-American relationship is in a state of transition.

A new generation is emerging and a number of social and cultural changes are under way that are also contributing to this transition. While our common heritage and values set limits on how far we may drift apart, there is an increasing recognition of the divergences between the United States and Europe on such critical issues as defense and arms control, policy toward the Soviet Union, East-West trade and technology transfer, West-West economic relations, North-South issues, and problems outside the NATO area. The challenge for statesmen will be to manage the differences—and where possible create a new Western consensus—in such a way as to enable the Alliance to adapt to new circumstances while preserving its basic character.

The relatively simple world of the postwar period is gone. Americans today appear to have less understanding of European perspectives and Europeans less appreciation of American views. There is much handwringing about the trans-Atlantic malaise, but less constructive thinking about how to manage and, where possible, reduce our differences.

The project is designed to identify and clarify the differences in interests and perspectives affecting critical issues in the European-American relationship, thereby enhancing understanding across the Atlantic. Approximately three issues per year are selected for examination on a rolling basis over a three-year period. The issues are those that are most likely to create friction in the period ahead.

A short book is published on each issue. European and American authors with points of view that differ from each other but represent important strands of thought in their respective societies contribute analyses of the problem and offer their policy prescriptions. We hope that by disaggregating the issues in this manner, we can make a constructive contribution to the Atlantic debate.

An advisory group of Council members, with the participation of European guests, helps to choose the issues and discusses the ideas in the manuscripts prior to publication. They are, however, in no way responsible for the conclusions, which are solely those of the authors.

We would like to thank the Rockefeller Foundation, the Andrew W. Mellon Foundation and the German Marshall Fund of the United States for their assistance in supporting this project.

Cyrus R. Vance

Advisory Group
Project on European-American Relations

The editor would like to thank James Chace, Mark Falcoff, William LeoGrande, Karl Meyer, Eusebio Mujal-Leon, Susan Purcell and John E. Sawyer for joining the Advisory Group in its discussions on this topic. He would also like to thank Anne Bertelsen, Andrea Giles, Norman Jacobs, David Kellogg, Rob Valkenier, and Alfred Zwiebel for their assistance in the production of this book.

The Project on European-American Relations is under the auspices of the Council's Studies Program.

Already published:
Nuclear Weapons in Europe, *edited by Andrew J. Pierre, with contributions by William G. Hyland, Lawrence D. Freedman, Paul C. Warnke and Karsten D. Voigt.*

Unemployment and Growth in the Western Economies, *edited by Andrew J. Pierre, with contributions by Marina v. N. Whitman, Raymond Barre, James Tobin and Shirley Williams, and an introduction by Robert D. Hormats.*

Contents

ix

About the Authors

Fernando Morán is the Spanish Minister of Foreign Affairs. In 1978 he was elected to the Senate and served there as the Socialist Party spokesman for foreign affairs until 1982. A career diplomat since 1954, Mr. Moran was Chief of Studies at the Spanish Diplomatic School from 1978 to 1982. In addition, he has held a number of positions in the Foreign Ministry including Political Director for Foreign Policy from 1970 to 1971; and Director General for Africa and the Middle East from 1976 to 1977. Mr. Moran has been posted in London as Consul General, in Lisbon as First Secretary, as well as in Pretoria and London. His publications include *Una politica exterior para Espana.*

Irving Kristol is co-editor of *The Public Interest.* He has been a member of the faculty at New York University since 1969, where he has held the title of Professor of Social Thought at the Graduate School of Business Administration since 1979. In addition, Mr. Kristol is currently a Senior Fellow at the American Enterprise Institute and a member of the President's Commission on White House Fellowships. Previously, he served as Executive Vice President of Basic Books from 1961 to 1969; Editor of *The Reporter* from 1959 to 1960; Co-editor (and Co-founder) of *Encounter* from 1953 to 1958; and Managing Editor of *Commentary* from 1947 to 1952. Mr. Kristol is the author of *Two Cheers for Capitalism* and *Reflections of a Neoconservative.*

Michael D. Barnes is a member of the U.S. House of Representatives from the state of Maryland and Chairman of the Subcommittee on Western Hemisphere Affairs of the House Foreign Affairs Committee. He served as a Senior Counsellor to the National Bipartisan Commission on Central America (Kissinger Commission) in 1983–84 and was Walter Mondale's representative to the National Democratic Platform Committee and spokesman on platform issues at the 1984 National Democratic Convention. Prior to his election to Congress, Mr. Barnes practiced law with the Washington firm of Covington & Burling from 1972 to 1975; served as Executive Director of the National Democratic Platform Committee for the Democratic National Convention in 1975–76; and was Special Assistant to Senator Edmund S. Muskie on the Muskie for President Committee from 1970 to 1972.

Alois Mertes is Minister of State in the Foreign Office of the Federal Republic of Germany and a member of the Bundestag. From 1980 to 1982 he was foreign affairs spokesman for the Christian Democratic Union/Christian Socialist Union parliamentary party and from 1972 to 1980 functioned as an expert on security policy for the same CDU/CSU group. In addition, Mr. Mertes served as deputy chairman of the CDU's Federal Committee on Foreign and German Affairs from 1975 to 1982 and as the Plenipotentiary of the Land of Rhineland Palatinate to the Federation in 1972. He has filled a number of positions in the West German foreign service including Head of Division (from 1969 to 1971) and Deputy Head of Division (from 1966 to 1968) for European Security and Regional Disarmament; First Secretary in the West German embassy in Moscow from 1963 tp 1966 and First Secretary in Paris from 1956 to 1958.

Daniel Oduber was President of Costa Rica from 1974 to 1978 and is currently Vice President of the Socialist International and a member of the Inter-American Dialogue. He co-founded the National Liberation Party in 1951 and was its president from 1970 to 1974. In addition, Mr. Oduber served as President of the Costa Rican Congress from 1970 to 1973; as Minister of Foreign Affairs from 1962 to 1964; as a member of Congress from 1958 to 1962; and as Special Ambassador to Europe from 1953 to 1955.

Andrew J. Pierre is a Senior Fellow at the Council on Foreign Relations and the Director of the Project on European-American Relations. Formerly on the staff of the Brookings Institution and the Hudson Institute, he has also taught at Columbia University. In addition, he served with the Department of State as a Foreign Service Officer in Washington and abroad. Mr. Pierre is the author of *The Global Politics of Arms Sales, Nuclear Politics: The British Experience with an Independent Strategic Force, Nuclear Proliferation: A Strategy for Control*, and other works.

Andrew J. Pierre

Introduction

The Third World, as it is commonly known, has become the most fluid and in some ways the most dangerous aspect of world politics. In contrast, the central strand that runs from the United States through Europe to the Soviet Union is relatively strong, stability being enhanced by nuclear deterrence and the armed confrontation of the two strongest military alliances in history. Unfortunate as this massive confrontation may be, and as susceptible to complex fine-tuning as the nuclear equation is, there is no denying that until now they have brought an important measure of stability to the central East-West balance. Instability, on the other hand, characterizes much of the Third World today.

For the developing world, political instability has often been a corollary to political change. (Its desirability depends of course upon the case at hand.) For developed countries, especially those with global interests and responsibilities, coping with the impact of such instability can present a major policy challenge. They must be sensitive to the fine line between unwarranted intervention in the affairs of other nations and the justifiable safeguarding of their own interests. As in the case of Central America, this requires nuanced judgment on complex and sensitive issues.

Given the pervasive nature of the East-West political competition, the question of whether a local or regional conflict does, or does not, have global ramifications almost invariably arises. Differences in analysis and differences in policy approaches are sure to abound. The authors of this book not only illustrate such differences within Europe and the United States with respect to Central America, but from their varying points of view they also make clear the dangers that policy disagreements on that region present for trans-Atlantic relations.

There have been approximately 140 conflicts since the Second World War, 95 percent of which have occurred in the Third

1

World. The reasons for such instability are varied and complex, but not unknown. Many states were artificial creations, enveloping peoples of differing races, religions and cultures. Economic and social tensions, often aggravated by poverty or even by the very process of development, have given rise to ethnic, religious and political conflict. Many times these tensions have led to internal strife. External conflict has been the result of territorial disputes or of competition of another sort with neighboring states, be it ethnic, economic, political or religious in origin.

A contributing factor to the growth of Third World instability was the disintegration of the colonial order in the years following World War II. In recent decades the erosion of the dominance of the superpowers has further contributed to the general pattern of fragmentation. This has been accompanied by a diffusion of military power with the creation or growth of national armed forces and a substantial acquisition of weapons and military capabilities on the part of Third World nations.

In the past it was possible for nations to be relatively disinterested in disturbances and conflicts that were far away. But this has become less and less possible. Because of such factors as the actual and potential proliferation of nuclear weapons, the interdependence of much of the world economy through the international trading system, and the global political competition between East and West, once "distant" developments are now perceived as much closer to home. In this process the revolutions in communication and transport have been central. Television and the media in general, the jet aircraft and the existence of rapid deployment military capabilities, have served to greatly compress distance and speed up time. Almost anything, anywhere around the globe becomes important if we choose to perceive it as such.

For outside powers whose interests are in some way affected by an instability in the Third World, the issue becomes: What is tolerable and what is intolerable? What is easily accepted and requires no reaction, and what is dangerously disturbing and calls for safeguarding one's interests through a planned response?

Judgments of this sort are difficult to reach under almost any circumstances. Often they must be made on the basis of imperfect knowledge, in a context that is dynamic rather than static. Political ideology and instincts may play a significant part. And in the current predicaments of world politics, such judgments about local or regional problems can rarely be divorced from the fundamental and continuing East-West political rivalry.

The Third World, it seems at times, has become a great arena for competition between the Soviet Union and the West. Among the Soviet-watchers there is disagreement on whether Moscow has been basically motivated by some global "grand design" to spread communism or has been more inclined to seize opportunities as they arise within the Third World. Yet one need not resolve the debate to identify some of the basic ingredients in Soviet policy. Clearly there is a significant ideological component whereby the Soviet Union supports Marxist-Leninist "movements of national liberation" and communist parties with varying degrees of commitment. But in addition, and related, to the ideological element is the political factor. Moscow seeks global political parity with the West. Its nuclear arms have given it a military parity which has not been translated into political status in the Third World. Hence the search for clear recognition as a superpower, for a legitimation in the eyes of much of the rest of the world, leads the U.S.S.R. to seek to expand its influence around the globe. Often a parallel objective, or consequence, is to undermine Western, particularly U.S., influence and interests.

Economic incentives are not unimportant. The U.S.S.R. is in need of hard currency and welcomes markets where it can be acquired as through the increasingly profitable sale of arms. The economic benefits that the Soviet Union reaps through its Third World policies still appear to be quite limited, however, and less significant than the ideological and political benefits. There are also important military and strategic considerations. The Soviet Union seeks bases in the Third World. It has steadily expanded its navy so as to exert influence far beyond its borders, though it has some way to go to match the United States in overall naval power. The U.S.S.R. also makes use of proxies, such as nationals of Cuba and several East European states, in its Third World activities.

Inevitably all this leads to competition, and sometimes confrontation, with the West. The West is committed to supporting democracies, but many of its citizens also subscribe to a further goal of containing communism. This has, at times, brought alignment with authoritarian regimes.

The original sources of instability and conflict in the Third World are often far removed from the East-West competition, as in the case of the Middle East. But the postwar experience has been that conflicts of any substantial importance do not readily play themselves out without involving powers external to the particular Third World region. Political relationships, geographic proximity, resource dependency, commercial links, and the provision of military facilities for allied states all serve to draw in nations external to the region.

Third World instability can destroy the relative—even if precarious—stability between the First and Second Worlds. This is one reason why it is so critical for Europe and the United States. The détente of the early 1970s died not because of a direct Soviet-American clash but because of the Western perception of Soviet behavior in the Middle East (the October War), Angola, and the Horn of Africa. Soviet-Cuban military intervention in the two African conflicts did much to foster a far more skeptical attitude toward the once widely accepted benefits of détente. Strategic arms control has also suffered from Third World instability. Afghanistan sealed the fate of the SALT II treaty, but its ratification had been compromised by the debate a few months earlier about a Soviet brigade in Cuba. Nor can one forget Zbigniew Brzezinski's remark about SALT II having been buried in the sands of the Ogaden.

There has been much controversy about the "linkage" between arms control and the overall climate of East-West relations. Whether or not such a linkage should be used as a foreign policy instrument is a debatable proposition. Less debatable is the conclusion that public perceptions of East-West conflict in Third World situations erode the support for arms control (as well as for economic cooperation with the East). In that sense, linkage is a political reality whether we like it or not. A major clash in Central America between Moscow and Washington, for example, could badly damage current arms control negotiations in Geneva.

Differences over whether and how to deal with specific cases of Third World instability can easily become a major problem in relations between European nations and the United States. The 1956 Suez crisis and the Vietnam War serve as useful reminders. Divisions over Central America are, as of now, not as deep, but the authors of this book note the potential for serious disagreement with lasting consequences. Fernando Morán, for example, observes that a massive U.S. intervention would strengthen neutralist and pacifist movements in Europe to such an extent that the continued participation in NATO of certain governments, especially Spain, would be jeopardized. Irving Kristol, on the other hand, states his belief that a major falling out between the United States and Europe over Central America could soon lead to overwhelming pressures in the United States for a redefinition of its role in NATO—even to the point of the withdrawal of U.S. forces from the European continent. There are of course other contrasting views, well represented here by Alois Mertes and Michael Barnes. In the Atlantic world the public debate now hardly ever pits European *versus* American views, but is more complex with segments of European opinion in parallel with counterparts in the United States. Daniel Oduber's contribution is an important reminder that, as seen from Central America, the Europeans have at times had, and should now continue to maintain, a special role in the region.

In the following pages the reader will find significant disagreements over the fundamental nature of the crisis in Central America; the policy of the United States; the role of external powers, such as the European nations, the Soviet Union and Cuba; the appropriate mix of foreign policy instruments in successfully dealing with the problem; and the possibility for negotiations. But there is little disagreement that the manner in which the United States deals with this situation in its "backyard" will affect its credibility as a world leader. Above all, *that* is what makes Central America a European-American issue.

Fernando Morán

Europe's Role in Central America: A Spanish Socialist View

The Central American crisis has intensified in recent years. Worldwide concern has increased about events in the region, especially about the risk that various conflicts there could evolve into a much broader confrontation with unforseeable consequences.

There has been substantial resistance in Europe to the Reagan Administration's appraisal of the situation, which views the region's problems mainly as a part of the global East-West conflict. Such a perception implies, in effect, that possible solutions to the crisis must be subordinated to the higher goals of global politics, a subordination that would also affect relations between Europe and Central America.

The resistance to current American policy, however, is not shared equally by all. It is colored not only by each European government's particular position on the ideological spectrum but also by the differing importance each country accords to Central America, as well as by the deteriorating international climate.

In this sense Spain seems to have become "pivotal." Because it has quite old and extensive relations with Central America, it is one of the countries that has more strongly resisted the subordination of its policies to general global concerns. Moreover, pending decisions about Spain's continued participation in the North Atlantic Treaty Organization (NATO) could affect global American policy and could, in turn, be affected by events in Central America. Finally, because of its understanding of the region and the proven reluctance of the government of Felipe González to let its policies be affected by ideological prejudices, Spain's views on Central America can have some degree of influence on other less concerned European governments.

From Spain's point of view, the Central American situation is very serious. In spite of periodic tranquilizing pronouncements,

U.S. policy over the past two years has responded to an interventionist logic. This is true even of its most positive aspects: for example, U.S. efforts to legitimize the Salvadoran regime and to limit human rights violations could, if the Salvadoran Army were to find itself in difficulty, make U.S. intervention easier. Similarly, the dialogue started in mid-1984 between Washington and the Sandinistas, if not accompanied by decisive advances in the Contadora peace process, runs the risk of transforming a regional effort into a bilateral negotiation that could break down at any moment.

In this essay I intend to elaborate on these issues which, to my mind, lie at the center of the European debate on Central America. Although I inevitably argue from a Spanish point of view, I have tried to reflect a reasoning that I believe is shared by a considerable number of other European governments and scholars.

I feel compelled to say from the outset that the Central American "case" seems to be a very special example of political instability in the Third World. This is because the term "Third World" as it is applied to any part of Latin America has always made me uncomfortable. These are countries that have been independent for more than 150 years, are a part of the Western Hemisphere, and are deeply, though not completely, penetrated by Western tradition and values. The virtues of using Central America as a "case study" stem from the fact that the prosperity and stability of the region are imperative and from what is perceived to be at stake there.

Over the last year it has often been stated that the security of the West is at stake in Central America. In my opinion, what is in jeopardy is perhaps even more important: the very definition and credibility of the West. Credibility is gained by defending friends, but it can be jeopardized by letting them run unnecessary risks and by disappointing and alienating those who could become friends.

I. Differences in European and American Perspectives on Central America

Many Europeans—European conservatives included—have resisted accepting the prevalent analysis in the United States that sees the current Central American crisis exclusively as one more manifestation of the East-West conflict.[1] This does not mean, as has often been suggested, that Europeans are indifferent to U.S. security concerns or "naive" about the true intentions of the "Managua-Havana-Moscow" axis. For obvious reasons related to Europe's geopolitical situation, its history, and its differing level of world responsibilities, Europe has a different perspective on what is happening on the isthmus and how it relates to the world situation. This is so even though for a number of years, as we will see below, the European view was to a large extent relatively close to the American interpretation—so long as the latter remained within what today seem "moderate" bounds.

Differences arose, or more accurately, sprang forth from the limited academic and political arena of the European left into governmental circles when, upon assuming office, the Reagan Administration made it perfectly clear that Central America was one of the keys to the U.S. effort to regain military superiority and political initiative throughout the world. Within this global "crusade," the recovery of North American influence in Central America and the Caribbean—undoubtedly eroded since the early 1960s—gradually became, and perhaps involuntarily so, the crucial testing ground for measuring the seriousness of the Republican Administration's intentions or, as is sometimes said, the "credibility" of its foreign policy.

It was evident that President Reagan was not going to illustrate his intentions with a mere rhetorical attack on the Soviet Union; so it became necessary to make it very clear that he would not hesitate to respond decisively in Nicaragua or El Salvador. To erase any doubts, Grenada was subsequently invaded. It is Washington's willingness to carry its policies in Central America to the limit of confrontation that has brought the differing perspectives of Europe and the United States to the surface. This can be seen

---

[1] In this respect, the final communiqué (see appendix) of the San José meeting of September 28–29, 1984, is revealing. The ten foreign ministers of the European Economic Community, plus Spain and Portugal agreed (along with the foreign ministers from the Contadora and Central American nations) on a basic analysis of the Central American problems and, among other considerations, ruled out military solutions.

today as much by what the European governments do not do, as by what they actually do. It can also be seen in Europe's unprecedented presence in the region. If these differences have not yet had grave repercussions in European-American and intra-European relations, it is because a military confrontation has not yet materialized.

The diagnosis and evaluation of the Central American crisis usually offered in Europe comes in different versions and various shades. It varies from country to country and according to the particular position of governments and parties on the political spectrum. Still, it is possible to emphasize a few basic, common ideas that underlie the European points of view.

The "Historic Failure" of U.S. Policy

European analysis probably accepts most of the traditional North American assumptions about U.S.-Central American-Caribbean relations, and, in particular, it has never questioned that the United States has fundamental strategic interests in the region. Nevertheless, for almost 20 years European thinking has revealed a quite clear appreciation of what I would venture to call North America's "historic failure" in Central America.

U.S. influence in Central America grew without interruption from the time the region achieved independence in the early 1800s, particularly since the acceleration of U.S. expansion following the war with Mexico in 1846-48. For a time this was compatible with Europe's considerable commercial and colonial presence in the region. U.S. interests then were, above all, economic and quasi-private to the extreme extent that in the 1850s William Walker, at his own expense and risk, conquered half of Nicaragua. Later—and especially after the Mexican Revolution of 1910 (which at one point was also accused of having Marxist support)—strategic interests became dominant. In the process American economic, political and military hegemony in the region was gradually established and was considerably strengthened as a result of the war with Spain in 1898. That war led to the annexation of Puerto Rico and the establishment in Cuba of what Cubans now call the "la República Mediatizada" (literally, the Controlled Republic), in which the United States' right to intervene was included in the nascent republic's constitution by way of the Platt Amendment.[2]

For six decades U.S. hegemony remained complete and unquestioned. Neither Europe, preoccupied with its own internal problems; nor the other Latin American countries, also divided and undergoing painful processes of political modernization; nor the inhabitants of Central America themselves, were in a position to challenge the United States. The region was considered implicitly or explicitly the sole concern of its dynamic neighbor to the North. Or to put it more crudely, the Central American republics became the United States' "backyard." This was, after all, in keeping with the tenor of the age. While the United States was consolidating its influence—a process that did not rule out military intervention—Europe was dividing up Africa and the East. But whereas by the middle of the twentieth century Europe had lost its colonial possessions as the outcome of a long process of withdrawal, nothing changed for the United States in its relationship with Central America and the Caribbean.

Oscillating between military intervention and neglect, and allied with local oligarchies, the United States made little contribution to the incipient processes of economic and social change in the region. For these processes might have adversely affected the "status quo" and therefore American political and economic interests.

The result is evident. On the whole, Central America is today, with the possible exceptions of the Bolivian altiplano and the Brazilian Northeast, the poorest region in Latin America. Social structures—always excepting Costa Rica's—more closely approximate colonial patterns than what one would expect to find in an area neighboring the richest country in the world. And today the Nicaraguan regime's rhetoric has more in common with some young African nations than with a country in which the colonial power quietly withdrew more than a century and a half ago.

The historical process that led to the contemporary Central American crisis is not well known in Europe. Nor, above all, is it

---

[2] The 1901 Platt Amendment to the U.S. Army appropriations bill stipulated the conditions for the withdrawal of U.S. troops from Cuba. In order to end the U.S. occupation, Cuba agreed to incorporate the amendment's articles in its constitution. The articles, among other things, granted the United States permission to intervene in Cuba "for the preservation of Cuban independence."

understood how the United States, which so decisively helped Europe to recover from the devastation of war, has been unable after more than a century to create stability and prosperity in a region so close to its own borders.

Today Europeans see the possibility that the United States, which has been unable to develop this tiny region it has always dominated—a region whose total area is about that of Texas and whose population barely surpasses that of the State of New York—may be tempted to resort to force.

There is another factor that aggravates and illustrates the historic failure of the United States and that contributes to increasing Europe's skepticism. That is Cuba, a case that most European politicians now in power have observed in the course of their public lives.

Speculation about whether Fidel Castro was or was not a communist in 1959, or about what would have happened if the United States had pursued different policies instead of the disastrous landing at the Bay of Pigs and the imposition of a trade embargo (which not even General Franco could support), is irrelevant. What is evident is that the United States lost all ability to influence politics on the island, and that 25 years later, the embargo has not weakened the Castro regime or forced it to renounce expansionary policies, but has strengthened its economic and military ties with the Soviet Union.

The embargo has hurt only the Cuban population, whose level of consumption today is not consistent with other indicators of its social development. If the Cuban revolution has lost prestige in Europe, it is certainly because of its own errors and as a result of its outworn propaganda. Yet even in this context, the Cuban regime, though mired in a pre-Stalinist revolutionary rhetoric that leads it to export teachers and doctors along with ideology and soldiers, has seen neither its ability to survive nor its dynamic foreign policy weakened. If this is the result of a quarter-century of economic strangulation and political isolation, one can hardly view U.S. policy toward Cuba as a success.

That U.S. policies toward Central America and the Caribbean have been a failure is, in my opinion, a fairly general perception in Europe. Herein lies the origin of European skepticism toward Washington's present policies, irrespective of the particular political and ideological assessments made by individual governments.

The situation today is particularly serious both for world politics and for the Atlantic Alliance. The radical policies enunciated by Washington, without precedent in the last 20 years, are superimposed upon a tense international situation and come at a difficult time for Europe. The invasion of Grenada in October 1983 was a clear signal that the United States would, if it deemed necessary, intervene militarily in the region without consulting its allies.

The U.S. approach perceives the fundamental root of the crisis in the global East-West conflict. Hence Americans deduce that the security of the United States, that is, of the West, is threatened. And as in any all-out war, anyone who does not see the problem in these terms either shows himself to be "soft" on vital questions of Western defense, or, worse, becomes what the Marxists call an "objective ally" of the enemy.

I am tempted to suggest—and I am well aware that I cannot represent the positions or opinions of Western Europe as a whole—that not many of the allied governments in Europe fully share this analysis. True, Europe's prudence and awareness of its own limitations, as well as its sincere desire not to exacerbate trans-Atlantic differences and "misunderstandings" in a moment as delicate as the present one, have limited open criticism to the most scandalous actions (such as the mining of Nicaraguan ports early in 1984), which were also widely criticized in the United States. Nevertheless, Europeans should not fail to observe that their actual support for the general U.S. approach has been very slight and, above all, unenthusiastic.

Joseph Luns, the former Secretary General of NATO, was correct in noting that Spain was the only country in the Alliance to "criticize energetically" the invasion of Grenada. But it is just as true that not one single European government supported it openly.

The Dimension of Underdevelopment

For the Spanish government, and for European Social Democratic governments in general (as well as for many Christian Democrats and Liberals),[3] the basic causes, the roots, of the different conflicts

---

[3] See the "Declaration on Latin America of the Three Party International Presidents" (Socialist, Christian Democratic and Liberal), Rome, April 10, 1984.

in the region lie in its underdevelopment: in the deplorable economic and social structures of the Central American countries (Costa Rica excepted), and in the models of political organization that have survived with few changes since the beginning of this century. (Indeed, the few changes that have occurred have been regressive ones, designed to confront growing challenges with ever more brutal repression.)

The economic and social situation in the region is well known. It cannot be explained, as it is in the National Bipartisan Commission on Central America (Kissinger Commission) report, as being an outgrowth of the structures created by Spanish colonialism, which are said to have remained unchanged over four centuries. The Salvadoran latifundia, for example, which form the basis of El Salvador's economic structure and are a source of political power, were created in the last third of the nineteenth century.

Apart from Costa Rica, whose unique history breaks all the rules and simultaneously gives hope to the rest of the region, the tragedy of Central America today is the result of the inability of its dominant classes to carry out or accept the reforms necessary for development. This inability was reinforced when—once American economic interests had acquired a stake in the region—the dominant classes succeeded in convincing governments in Washington that to defend them was to defend the United States. In very general terms one can say that, thanks to its lack of concern for the region, the United States allowed itself to be used for many years by regimes that, whether on a family basis (the Somozas) or an institutional one (alliance of the oligarchy and the military in El Salvador), eliminated all possibility of development, moderniza tion or democracy.

The 1960s were for Central America, as for most of the world, years of economic expansion. The Central American economies, despite their great structural weaknesses, not only took advantage of U.S. economic aid programs such as those implemented by the Alliance for Progress, but also multiplied the benefits of the boom by creating their own mechanisms for economic integration, such as the Central American Common Market. Political developments, however, were not good. The traditional elites survived, thanks to their alliances with the military and systematic use of electoral fraud. Still, there were two very positive developments. On the one hand, following the events in the Dominican Republic in 1965, the very long period of "automatic intervention" that had characterized the first half of the century appeared to come to a close. On the other hand, economic growth offered hope not only to the emerging middle classes but even to underprivileged social and economic groups. This led them to believe that economic development would absorb social tensions and facilitate the reforms that very broad moderate sectors already judged absolutely necessary.

During the 1970s it became more apparent that growth—undercut by generally decreasing world prosperity as well as by a crisis in the Central American Common Market—would not be sufficient to change archaic economic structures in the region. Moreover, as a result of the great convulsions of the previous decade (the Cuban revolution, the success of African and Asian liberation movements, the war in Vietnam, and Vatican II), popular and nationalistic movements acquired unprecedented strength throughout Central America. It is impossible to say to what extent the mystique of "Ché" Guevara or the less mythical members of the Tricontinental Solidarity Organization (which was founded in 1967 to promote Marxist national liberation movements in Africa, Asia and Latin America), were responsible for the emergence of these groups; it is also politically irrelevant. Many began to perceive and recognize openly the necessity for change, and this includes not just Social Democrats or Christian Democrats but also pure liberals. The fact is that the urgent need to broaden the spectrum of political participation, to carry out agrarian and economic reforms, and to respect the most elemental human rights of populations began to be felt throughout Central American society, including in the middle and upper-middle classes.

In very little time these various groups, not always guerrilla movements but also labor unions, political parties and religious organizations, gained force, awakening hopes for real change throughout the isthmus. For the first time in years, these hopes appeared to be understood by Washington. Between 1977 and 1979 events of such transcendence as the signing of the Panama Canal Treaties, the fall of Anastasio Somoza Debayle in Nicaragua, and the assumption of power by the reformist junta in El Salvador took place. There was even a small opening between Cuba and the United States, which allowed Europeans to think that all might change in the region. Only in Guatemala was change blocked by an increase in repression. Neighboring countries, particularly Mexico, Panama and Venezuela, applauded these changes and encouraged the new governments.

However, in a very short time—barely months—these hopes came tumbling down. In the early 1980s it became obvious that the Central American region had entered one of the harshest and most terrible periods of its history. The Nicaraguan revolution quickly broke its mold and beginning in 1981, when it proclaimed its support for the Salvadoran guerrillas and eliminated representatives of the liberal middle class from its leadership structures, became a destabilizing force in the region. In El Salvador the military's reaction to the junta's reforms was so brutal that half of the junta abandoned the government to join the guerrillas. The country has since been consumed by civil war.

In Panama Omar Torrijos Herrera's heir was expelled by the military. In Guatemala the regime outdid itself in its blind repression that affected moderates and Christian Democrats as much as peasants and priests. And the incipient U.S. dialogue with Cuba also soon came to a dead end.

The backdrop for this general convulsion has been an economic decline that is carrying the region to such dramatic levels of underconsumption and decapitalization as to render any hope of development illusory. Debt is the major problem only in Costa Rica; in the rest of the region the problem is survival.

Washington's policies, as has been noted, had much to do with the changes in 1978 and 1979 (for which former Vice President Walter Mondale was strongly criticized during the 1984 presidential election campaign). But Washington had perhaps an even stronger impact when the "hard-line" theses, so clearly articulated by U.N. Ambassador Jeane J. Kirkpatrick and so skillfully rationalized in the Kissinger Commission report, were applied by the Reagan Administration.

For this reason we cannot limit our analysis to North-South issues, no matter how convinced we may be that underdevelopment and its causes lie at the root of the problem. If Central America today is a powder keg of unpredictable range and not simply a regional battleground, it is because of the region's geopolitical position, a fact neither Spain nor any other country can ignore. The geopolitical dimension is clearly at the center of Washington's policies toward Central America.

The Geopolitical Dimension

In the first months of 1981 Washington reoriented its policies toward Central America. As a result, these new policies became one more element contributing to the crisis. From the outset of the Reagan Administration, when it identified the problems in the region as part of the global confrontation, Washington's major goal became the isolation and neutralization of Nicaragua through an increased political, and especially military, presence in the region. The Administration demonstrated its resolve to never again restrict U.S. involvement in Central America's affairs or to permit "the loss" of another country in the region. Accordingly, in Honduras the United States combined an unprecedented military deployment with aid to the nascent constitutional government. In El Salvador it linked important military assistance (intended to enable the army to confront a guerrilla movement that had grown extraordinarily stronger politically) to limited democratization of the regime (limited in that it hardly touched the real bastions of power). In Nicaragua it started a barely concealed program of covert aid to the "contra" guerrillas that was coupled with direct dialogue only in mid-1984. And finally, it applied very strong pressures on Costa Rica to abandon its traditional neutrality.

There were also a number of attempts throughout 1983 to resurrect the old Central American military alliance, which failed, one would assume, in part because it was impossible to exclude Nicaragua from a treaty to which it was unquestionably a party. All these steps, along with the systematization of large-scale military maneuvers and the decisive invasion of Grenada, finally convinced the world that the United States would not hesitate to resort to force if events in the region made it "necessary."

In short, in a context of increasing militarization, aspirations for reform and democratization were once again subordinated to global stategic objectives. Although in El Salvador there have been some improvements, in general militarization has meant strengthening the region's most intransigent social classes as well as their domestic political agents, the military establishments, especially in El Salvador, Guatemala and Honduras.

Throughout the last four years Europe has provided scant support for Washington's policies. Although some European governments have frozen their aid to Nicaragua, the majority of them, particularly those that are socialist, neither support the "contras" nor favor ostracizing the Sandinistas. Except from the most conservative European governments, support for the present leaders of El Salvador is still unenthusiastic and is conditioned upon progress in peace negotiations. Yet, no European government today and very few important political parties deny that the Central American isthmus and Caribbean region are of primary strategic importance to the United States not only because it is a great power with global responsibilities, but also because it is a Western Hemisphere nation with the right to ensure its own security.

Nor are there any doubts about the real problems (including security-related ones) that the United States faces because of the presence of a Soviet ally only a few miles from its coast, and because another country crucially located on the isthmus has undergone a spectacular reversal in its domestic and foreign policies since 1979. There is a more or less clearly expressed consensus in Europe that the United States is an important factor—from a political, economic and security standpoint—in the future of Central America.

However, various European governments, beginning with the Spanish government—whose views on this particular matter are taken more seriously in Europe than on other matters of common interest, for reasons to be explained below—do question that the global, East-West strategy approach can explain in any depth the problems of the region. They also question whether this approach can provide the means to find and apply a lasting solution to them, one which would deactivate the explosive potential of the region's problems. On the contrary, it seems quite clear to many Europeans that the global approach and the policies derived from it have contributed in a signficant way to exacerbating the existing conflicts and even to creating some new ones—for example, the increasing political instability in Honduras and Costa Rica.

Europeans must also note that, after the experience of decolonization, which culminated in the 1960s with the enthusiastic support of the United States, no one in Europe any longer questions the rights of peoples to self-determination, to the form of government they choose; to full national and social development; and to respect for their countries' sovereignty and territorial integrity, regardless of geographic location. When these principles are not respected—as happened in Afghanistan at the beginning of this decade—the entire world, starting with Europe and Latin America, rises in unanimous condemnation.

Nor is this stance due to "Europe's guilty conscience" vis-à-vis the Third World (as is sometimes said in the United States) or is it a case of "moral posturing." Rather it reflects factors that have considerable political weight in different European countries.

From the viewpoint of Europeans on the left, including the Spanish government, there is little hope that Washington's policies will succeed. As long as economic power continues to be concentrated in the hands of agrarian oligarchies that are more willing to live off interest from their dollars banked in Miami than to invest in their own countries, as long as the mass of the population remains on the margins of politics, and as long as armies continue to grow and absorb economic resources and decision-making power, the reforms that are needed will never cease to appear radical and almost revolutionary in character.

No doubt the elections held in El Salvador in May 1984 have contributed to shifting the North American public's attention from El Salvador to Nicaragua. In Spain's view the elections do represent an important step that could open the door to peace in El Salvador. But however important Nicaragua may be, the problem of Central America is not only Nicaragua. I would even go so far as to say that despite all its hasty and sometimes thoughtless actions, the Sandinista regime has resolved, without excessive trauma, some very serious problems—for example, the question of agrarian reform—that its neighbors have yet to address. At the same time, of course, it has created other problems. However Marxist-Leninist some of its leaders may be, Nicaragua's problem is that it is geographically, culturally and politically a Western country and should continue to be so, because that is probably what the majority of its population wants. Mining its ports, bombing its airports, and attacking its border towns with mercenaries, however, does not seem to me the best way to convince them.

Nicaragua is just as far (but no farther) from achieving the social reconciliation that would permit its citizens the full exercise of civil liberties as are El Salvador or Guatemala. It will be just as hard to "demilitarize" the Nicaraguan regime—with all that this implies for the security of the region—as it will be to liquidate the political role of the Salvadoran Army. And that will be even harder if Salvadoran President José Napoleón Duarte lets himself be tempted by a military solution, now that he seems to have less difficulty in obtaining the military aid required to do so. In this regard, Duarte's dramatic start of a political dialogue in late 1984 with the rebel forces in El Salvador and the army's involvement in this endeavor is a very optimistic development. The move was very warmly received in Europe, with the hope that American support for this effort at reconciliation would continue.

The need for reconciliation explains why Europeans, especially the Social Democrats, pushed so hard for meaningful conservative participation in the Nicaraguan elections in November 1984. And reconciliation also explains why Europe has always believed in a comprehensive, negotiated solution—one in which security and democratization are demanded of all groups and in which U.S. policies leave ample room for carrying out the reforms without which there can be no stability and development in the region.

In addition to these internal and geopolitical considerations, still other factors must be taken into account. These are the problems that stem from national aspirations and the regional perspective.

The National Dimension

The reason it has been so easy for guerrilla movements to gain strength in Central America is not simply the region's weak political structures or the efforts of a nearby revolutionary power, however significant and skillful these may be. The area's revolutionary potential has been greatly increased by the forces of nationalism that have matured in a historical situation with many semi-colonial characteristics.

The Cuban revolution's expansionary strength is based less on the success of its social system than on the fact that the revolution has given reality to the Cuban people's national identity and to their long struggle for national self-affirmation. Something similar, despite the differences, occurred with the Mexican Revolution in the first two decades of this century. And, to my understanding, nationalism is today the most dynamic mobilizing factor in the complex situation in Nicaragua. At this stage in history it should be obvious that unfulfilled nationalism carries a far more powerful revolutionary potential than does Marxist-Leninist doctrine, and it goes without saying that revolutionary movements are perfectly aware of this. Thus their rhetoric is far more nationalistic (and anti-American) than communist, whether in the appropriation of national myths (José Martí, Sandino, Farabundo Martí etc. . . .) or in the need for "the enemy" to be external (or, at least, a puppet of outsiders) and not some specific domestic social class.

The molding process of Central American and Caribbean nationalities has been complex. Except in Cuba, there was little, if any, fighting before independence. In any case, among the people of the region there was very little sense of belonging to the Central American Confederation (which took over the old territories of the former "Capitania General" of Guatemala consisting of present-day Costa Rica, El Salvador, Guatemala, Honduras and Nicaragua). Nor did a sense of national identity develop later on when the small disarticulated Central Amerian states were established, their borders determined more by the limits of each local caudillo's power than by the specific personality of each people. However, during the second half of the nineteenth century and the early twentieth century, conflicts between the different states on the one hand, and the growing North American presence on the other, sowed the seeds that bore fruit following the success of African and Asian movements in the 1960s. The national bourgeoisies and oligarchies, totally immune to this ferment, continued to believe for a long time that the United States would resolve all their problems. They convinced Washington that it was essential to support not only their specific interests but their political systems as well. As a result, Central American nationalism developed a two-sided character: first, contrary to what may occur among some sectors in Peru, for example, it is exclusively anti-American rather than anti-Spanish; second, in contrast to what occurrred in Europe, Latin American nationalism is neither bourgeois nor middle class but popular because the bourgeoisie identifies fundamentally with the "external agent" that protects it, that is, with the United States.

The Kissinger Commission report asserts that the United States must assume that any change, even revolutionary change, does not necessarily threaten the security of the United States. That is true. Still, taking existing circumstances into account, any change in Central America, and certainly any revolutionary change, will implicitly carry with it a certain dose of anti-Americanism so long as Washington's policies can be presented as an obstacle to national aspirations. That is why a fruitful relationship, one that can contribute to democratization and progress in the nations of Central America, must begin by accepting the need of these countries for national self-affirmation. That in turn means accepting a certain degree of anti-Americanism, which in all probability will be outgrown in later phases of the struggle for national self-assertion.

This growing awareness of national identity seems to have first been felt by the left, because the traditional right was linked to American interests. But nationalism is on the rise everywhere; it has made formidable progress in recent years, and I predict it will not stop here. In the first place, there are the armies. A small army that functions more as the personal guard of a dictator than as a national army may not be nationalistic. Somoza's Guardia Nacional clearly was not. But an army like that which is being built in El Salvador, which has doubled in number in the past two or three years and whose expansion continues at an accelerated pace, sooner or later will become nationalistic. And when it does, it will adopt for itself many of the political positions of the nationalist left. To some extent that is what occurred in Panama in the late 1960s, and in Peru at about the same time, though, in each case there were specific reasons for what happened as well.

Secondly, the national bourgeoisies are also feeling the pressures of nationalism, and this is the point at which the Central American crisis is linked directly to Latin America's general problems. The connecting point is the economic crisis and, in particular, the financial crisis that has pushed the continent to the edge of general bankruptcy. The austerity programs imposed by the International Monetary Fund, which many Latin Americans see as reflecting Washington's desires, will soon drive a number of moderate, democratic governments to the political graveyard. Those in the middle classes who do not emigrate are growing ever poorer, and their faith in the American way of life cannot help but be weakened. Their nationalistic reaction could be very strong.

The Regional Focus

However much it may seem when one reads the North American press, the United States and Central America do not exist by themselves in a geographic vacuum. There are two regional powers in the area in the classic sense: Mexico and Cuba. Each has its own economic, political and security concerns and an influence that could be called strong in the politics of the Central American countries. Mexico has a long history of influence in the region. Indeed, its importance is such that the Central American countries' fear of being absorbed by Mexico perhaps is what influenced their governments to appeal to the United States. Cuba is important, especially since the revolution, not only as an expansionary revolutionary power but also as a country that defends its own interests, and has significant security problems that determine its policies.

In the Cuban case (though this is speculation), not having normal relations with the countries of the area may well have made its influence as a revolutionary power greater than it would have been had Cuba had economic interests and trade to defend.

There are also two other regional powers with some responsibility in the Caribbean and with interests in Central America: Colombia and Venezuela. Nor can Panama be forgotten. Although in many ways Panama is also a Central American country, for some time it has played an interesting intermediary role among the different factions in the region. This is due to the particular skill of its leadership as well as the great prestige General Torrijos enjoyed throughout the region and the Hemisphere. By peaceful means and through negotiations, Torrijos obtained a treaty that in the eyes of a good many Latin Americans is a symbol of Panama's coming of age.

Colombia and Venezuela, after overcoming enormous difficulties, have both been able to establish functioning democratic regimes. If respect for life and human rights is not an absolute reality in both countries, it is at least built into their political structures and growing stronger. For them, as for Mexico, stability in Central America is vital.

Finally, the region includes the remnants of French and British colonialism in the Caribbean; Belize on the mainland, which was until recently a British colony and whose existence has contributed to Guatemala's isolation; and a rosary of unstable microstates created by British decolonization. The latter are a permanent source of instability since they can easily disintegrate politically.

All this forms an extraordinarily complex regional situation. In general, all the states of the area are interested in seeing regional prosperity and stability develop as a means of protecting their own security and political systems. That includes Cuba, which is perfectly aware that a "Grenada" on the mainland would have incalculable repercussions for its own security. All see the growing militarization of the area as potentially explosive.

Nevertheless, obviously there are nuances. Still perceived as an "outlaw," Cuba lives, because of its marginal status and because it is objectively threatened, with a permanently accepted degree of risk that makes abandoning its "destabilizing" role difficult. It has always tried to control at least part of the surrounding Caribbean, though with little success (Jamaica, Grenada), and it will undoubtedly continue to offer aid and try to influence other states and political movements in the region.

The Contadora Group

Four countries (Mexico, Venezuela, Colombia and Panama) have so many common interests in the region that they have come together in the Contadora Group, which since January 1983 has taken over the constellation of peace initiatives squandered in 1981 and 1982. It has established a mechanism for regional mediation that in the past two years has become at least as decisive as American policy in the area.

The Contadora process has so successfully brought the regional approach into the analysis that it can no longer be ignored. Its message is clear: what has permitted unity among the four Contadora governments is not so much a common vision of the crisis as an important difference with the United States' approach and policy, even though the Contadora countries do share some of its goals, especially the need for containing the Soviet and Cuban presence on the continent.

Other factors that have made it possible for the Contadora Group to come together are the fear that the conflicts might become increasingly militarized, which could put an end to the fragile democracies in Honduras and Panama, and the fear that the doors to reform and social reconciliation in El Salvador and Guatemala could be definitely closed, and the fear that even the stability of demilitarized Costa Rica could be threatened. All this would have unavoidable repercussions, difficult to foresee but probably very serious, in Mexico, Colombia and Venezuela.

Contadora has been decisive on another level as well. It has weakened the global and military approach and has significantly influenced European positions on Central America over the last two years, making it possible for the Europeans to express their disagreements with the United States gracefully. Contadora's moral strength in 1983 and 1984 has been such that the Reagan Administration has not been able to dismiss it at any point, though the Administration did ignore Contadora for a considerable time and has put growing obstacles in its path.

Nevertheless, the underlying problems do not appear near solution because, as is often stated, there can be no solution in Central America without Washington or against Washington. Therefore, even though the Contadora process could resolve many of the real security problems that the crisis presents, it cannot respond to the desire to recover the political and military initiative that is the basis of the Reagan Administration's analysis. Hence, if the focus and objectives of American policy toward the region do not change, it will be very difficult for Contadora to bring peace to the region without the support of the United States.

Finally, the Contadora Group has been important because it has established intense and continuous negotiations among the Central American countries, negotiations that were unthinkable only two years ago. It has created a curious solidarity among the leaders, an awareness of their common interests, and some mechanisms for reducing the tensions of the all-too-frequent border crises, thus making escalation more difficult.

I sensed at the Costa Rica meeting that this strongly impressed the European ministers, who perhaps had expected to see manifestations of hostility among neighbors or a general rejection of Nicaragua by the other countries.

Whatever happens in the future, whether the revised treaty is signed or not, Contadora has already played a key role, not only by preventing decisions that would be irreversible, but also by providing an extraordinarily efficient mechanism for decreasing overall tension in the region.

Europeans do not deny that the United States has a role to play in Central America, nor that it would be good to reduce Cuba's presence in Nicaragua. What is questioned is whether analyzing the problem in global East-West terms will lead to a lasting solution for the region, or whether, to the contrary, such an approach may contribute to an exacerbation of the problems, and even threaten general stability.

The solution will necessarily have to respect the conflicting interests—but all of them, not just some. It will have to find ways to unleash the potential for economic development, which will require quasi-revolutionary social and political reforms, particularly if the West continues to believe in the importance of respecting human rights. It will have to find formulas that safeguard the global balance of power, that do not threaten security (not just of the United States but of all the states in the region), and that assure the real exercise of each state's sovereignty and the fulfillment of each people's national aspirations.

I believe sincerely that this is what the Contadora process has tried to do. That is why, when compared with all the fleeting attempts that preceded it, Contadora has gone so far and evoked so much support.

Finally, we must ask: What will happen if Contadora fails? That is a possibility we simply cannot dismiss. What will happen if Nicaragua goes beyond the "point of no return," which some of its leaders seem to want and others to fear? Or, what will happen if Duarte is not able to expand his base of support and is forced to cede political power to the army and the extreme right? What if the limited capacity of a small country like Honduras to absorb a large military presence is surpassed?

There are no easy answers to these questions. But Honduras, El Salvador and Costa Rica, though they want stronger security provisions in the Contadora Treaty, are just as afraid of direct intervention—an intervention that in no way would spare them—as Nicaragua is. It also seems that Sandinista extremism is a minority position in the newly elected government of Daniel Ortega Saavedra. There appears to be, as well, a growing perception in the government and among the rebels in El Salvador that an arrangement, though not necessarily a power-sharing one, is feasible in the not-too-unforeseeable future.

This means that negotiations have to go on. It is in any case very unlikely that Europeans will unconditionally accept the conclusions derived from Washington's hard-line. Europe borders on the East, and its perspective about what is and what is not a security threat cannot be the same. Moreover, Europe will always reject solutions that both increase the risk of global confrontation and undermine the moral foundations of the West.

II. Europe's Role in Central America

In contrast to what is often argued, Europe's interest in Central America is not a recent development. The adoption of policy positions on Central American affairs; the frantic activities of European political parties over the last few years, particularly those of the Socialist International; the European foreign ministers' meeting in Costa Rica, are all symptoms of what is obviously an increasing interest, though not one that is either novel or new.

During the years following World War II a divided and weakened Europe had only enough energy for its own reconstruction, which needed American aid. But France, Great Britain and The Netherlands had colonies in Central America and the Caribbean that, unlike those in other parts of the world, suffered no changes as a result of the war. And although over the next two decades Europe was busy "tending its own garden," it never wholly neglected the Latin Amerian world.

From the mid-1960s onward it became evident that there was interest in what was happening in Latin America. Both right-wing nationalists, like France's Charles de Gaulle, and the left, which had been traumatized first by decolonization and then by Vietnam and was permeated by theories of imperialism, became increasingly concerned with the region.

Europe's permanent interests in Central America, the favorable economic situation, and the fact that as the United States increased its presence in other parts of the world (Southeast Asia, the Middle East, etc.) it tended to become less active in Central America, all contributed to a gradually expanding network of European economic, cultural and political interests and ties with Central America. At the same time the political influence of the European democracies also gradually increased.

In the early 1970s two parallel phenomena occurred. On the one hand, the European economic recovery gave rise to a growing need to expand economically to other areas of the world. Latin America, with its eternal unexploited potential and its relatively developed infrastructure and human resources, became a favorite terrain for European investment and commerce. Although Central America was never important in this sense, it did perhaps obtain some marginal benefits. On the other hand, political parties in Europe, particularly the socialists but the Christian Democratic parties also, gradually became aware of new ideas concerning development and broadened their philosophical interest to the Third World. As a result, they sought increasingly to associate with parties and groups of similar ideology outside Europe.

This complex network of causes produced an increase of contacts between European political parties and Latin America. The phenomenon, well known and equally well documented, was particularly notable in the case of the Socialist International. The Nicaraguan revolution—indeed, the entire sequence of events toward the end of the 1970s—contributed powerfully to attracting the attention and interest of Europeans.

In 1982 an additional reason for this interest developed: for a moment the Malvinas War looked like it might damage relations between Europe and Latin America irreparably. However, its consequences seem to have been relatively well contained. Following the war, Europeans began a new wave of contacts and initiatives directed to recover Europe's traditional image of being open to cooperation with the Third World and respectful of its aspirations.

Two additional aspects are very important: first, concrete interest in Central America has increased in some West European countries as a result of contacts with Latin American nations, which have themselves been pursuing their own specific policies toward Europe for some time. In this sense the case of Mexico and France is particularly illustrative. Second, not only have the Central American countries been receptive to increasing contacts with Europe, they have sought them actively. The most recent example is the President of Costa Rica's European tour in the summer of 1984, which gave rise to the San José meeting.

However, this strengthening of economic, cultural and political ties between Europe and Central America and the consequent increase in European influence, did not mean disagreement with U.S. views until the situation became more critical, particularly after 1981.

The Sandinista regime not only hardened its positions but openly worked for rebel victory in El Salvador when in late 1980 the "final offensive" seemed near and both right-wing and guerrilla violence soared. The Central Intelligence Agency's financing and organization of the "contras," the militarization of Honduras, and border episodes colored an increasingly worrisome picture. Around this time, the socialists rose to power in France. Until then the questioning of American policy in Europe had been limited to critical seminars among aspiring comrades of the Socialist International or to the position of governments that were culturally very distant from Latin America, such as Sweden and West Germany (even though the role of the Social Democratic Party had been crucial). With the election of a socialist government in France in May 1981, such critical positions threatened to become the policies of the most important states in Europe. The Franco-Mexican declaration of August 1981 marked the emergence of this new context. With the election of Felipe González in Spain (without doubt since 1978 the European politician most familiar with Central America and best known in the region), the "front" of political leaders dissenting from American policy began to extend throughout Europe.

Paradoxically, it was precisely at this point that the new American policy pushed European governments to take an even greater interest in the Central American crisis. Undoubtedly Washington did not intend such an effect, but it was a logical outcome of the

Reagan Administration's determination to make the region one of the neurological centers of the East-West confrontation.

Europe Has No Strategic Interests, But. . .

Indeed, one of the reasons that had hitherto kept the European presence in the region at relatively low levels was the obvious fact that Europe, unlike the United States, had no vital strategic interests in Central America, except the defense of its colonial possessions (a factor nowadays practically limited to France).

But, now faced with U.S. determination to define the conflict as part of the global confrontation, Europe is directly affected in three ways: first, Europe is a part of the West and neither in Central America nor anywhere else can the United States arrogate to itself the sole representation of Western interests. Taking into account the specific acts that the United States has carried out in its struggle against "enemy" penetration in Central America—the financing and arming of mercenary armies that attack sovereign nations; the violation of sovereignty and the right of free navigation by mining ports; preventive military intervention; military and economic support for regimes that systematically violate human rights, etc.—Europe is directly affected because it is the very definition of the West that is at stake. As the Chairman of the Spanish Congressional Foreign Affairs Commission, Miguel Angel Martínez, said recently, "We Spaniards are not part of the West for geographical reasons. We belong to the West because we feel that the values which underlie the way of life and the political systems of the West are superior to all others; and we believe that by mining ports, financing armies of 'contras' and supporting regimes which allow 'death squads,' one is not defending the West, but rather undermining its foundations. In the end military power becomes infinitely vulnerable to the assault of morality and truth."[4]

Second, Europe is affected because the military, naval, land and air deployment that has been carried out in Central America, particularly over the last two years, could affect Western defense

---

[4]Speech made in Santander, Spain, July 1984.

capabilities on other fronts, such as in Europe itself or in the Persian Gulf. This possibility is sufficiently disturbing to preoccupy the European countries.

Europe is affected for yet a third reason. In spite of frequent declarations to the contrary, the logic of American policy suggests that if the methods used until now do not produce the desired result—if the guerrillas in El Salvador are not contained, if the isolation of Nicaragua results in increasing ties with Cuba and the Soviet Union—a large-scale military intervention might be "necessary."

There is an element here of what might be called "the Malvinas illusion," which has undoubtedly contributed to poisoning the situation. Yet the superpowers should never forget the corollary of their almost infinite military strength. As their military power increases, they lose the freedom to use it. However limited they may wish their actions to be, these will always affect the overall balance as well as the identity and definition of the bloc they represent. Because of its global responsibilities, the United States has probably less freedom to act militarily, even to protect its immediate security, than Israel has in its area, or Great Britain has to defend its colonial possessions.

I do not believe it is advisable for me to dwell excessively on the possibilities of armed intervention, as much for reasons of mental well-being as for the political prudence required by my official role as Foreign Minister of an allied European country. The United States is perfectly aware of the immediate consequences a massive military intervention would have on the security of Europe and other parts of the world. Perhaps sufficient thought has not been given to the consequences such an action might have in Central America itself and in the rest of Latin America. On the isthmus it would provoke an anti-American reaction and a diaspora of the guerrillas that would affect every country in the area, from Mexico to Panama. In the rest of Latin America it could irreversibly compromise not only the effort to achieve social peace in Colombia, but also the fragile democracies of Argentina, Peru and Bolivia, as well as the barely initiated transitions to civilian rule in Uruguay and Brazil.

On the European scene, massive intervention would strengthen neutralist and pacifist movements to such an extent that it could jeopardize the continued participation in NATO of some of its members, especially Spain.

Consequently, for all these reasons, Washington's policy has become, as the expression has it, "a self-fulfilling prophecy." The U.S. determination to make the Central American crisis a crucial part of the total East-West confrontation has thrust Europe, quite apart from its traditional links to Central America, into the center of the conflict.

During the last few years Europe has won new prestige in Central America, in part because of its own constructive efforts, but also in part as a by-product of the eroding image of the United States and its loss of influence. This is another "paradoxical result" of Washington's policy.

The United States has lost influence in the region for three reasons: first, the decreasing level of economic aid and cooperation brought about by the Reagan Administration. The effort to make increased militarization compatible with savings in economic aid is not easy, nor does it generally produce positive results.

Second, excessive American political interventionism has its price. Not only did over-emphatic support almost cost Duarte the elections; it is also beginning to create symptoms of unrest in Honduras.

And finally, American influence has perhaps declined because European discontent with the way the West is defended also affects Central American democrats, who are increasingly disturbed at the prospect of being pawns in a chess game or possibly corpses on a battlefield.

What Can Europe Do?

What can Europe do? The question is repeated in every intergovernmental meeting and seminar of experts.

Besides contributing economically to development once the peace process is solidly under way, Europe has a triple role to play. First, it can continue to offer an image of the democratic and Western world which is non-dominating and respectful of the national and social aspirations of the peoples of Central America. Western-style democracy cannot continue to be an exclusive entertainment of "upper class" nations, rather like the game of bridge, which the Latin Americans can enjoy only when there are no important interests that get in the way. As I have already argued, in a strict sense Latin America is not the Third World. Latin countries are not young nations still adapting to independent life, with almost insuperable problems of infrastructure and human capital. They are Western countries whose people largely share Western values, whose now lengthy history reflects their desire for a life of freedom, and whose material and human resources ought to permit full economic prosperity and political democracy. Europe has not only the right but the obligation to demand and do everything in its power to keep the peoples of Latin America, and more urgently of Central America, from becoming irreparably disillusioned with the West.

In the second place, Europe, which has played an essential role in the moral and cultural formation of the Latin American peoples, has an obligation to make every possible effort to ease tensions and to deflate situations that have been exacerbated for too long. The U.S. political system is peculiar in that it offers few opportunities to become familiar with Marxist language and literature. That is not the case in Europe, where parties and other groups that define themselves as Marxist are a part, and sometimes an important part, of local politics. Thus there is perhaps a role to be played in "translating" political language, which some particularly well-placed countries, such as Mexico and Colombia, are already playing and to which Europe could certainly make a positive contribution.

Third, so long as the narrow margin for maneuver that still exists is not reduced further, there is also perhaps room for Europe to build bridges to the most radical countries and movements in the region, the ones that are most opposed to what the West represents and without whom no solution will be lasting.

The most recent—and the most spectacular—European initiative in dealing with Central America's problems was the September 1984 meeting in Costa Rica, which was attended by the foreign ministers of the ten European Economic Community countries, plus Spain and Portugal (as well as by the foreign ministers of the Central American and Contadora nations). In reflecting on that meeting, a few additional thoughts come to mind.

Europe can foster the process of Central American integration, as it did in Costa Rica, by pressing for a multilateral organization with sufficient authority and support to make real decisions as a precondition for broad cooperation with the EEC.

Europe can also give its unanimous backing, as it already has, to the Contadora process. This support would make it harder, as I stated to the Spanish press when I returned from San José, for those involved to resort to force in order to solve existing problems.

Finally, Europe can send a very clear message to Washington expressing its unanimous support for a negotiated solution and rejecting, as was done implicitly in San José, suggestions for isolating Nicaragua and singling it out as the sole factor responsible for all the ills of the region.[5] In this sense the contrast between the San José declaration and President Reagan's speech to the United Nations barely three days earlier is very revealing.

Other Countries Outside the Region

Central America's ties to the nations of the southern part of the Hemisphere have never been very close. Nevertheless, the events of the last decade—and particularly the chain of military dictatorships throughout the continent that espoused the doctrine of "national security"—curiously served to bring some of these countries closer to Central America. The Southern Cone dictatorships broke all the unwritten rules of the Latin American political tradition, which imply some degree of respect for the integrity of institutions and individuals even under military rule. They applied repressive methods that had not been seen in the Western world since the fall of Nazism. And they did so precisely in the name of Western values. Some even acted beyond their own frontiers, as when the Argentine military came to "advise" the second Salvadoran junta and the armies of other countries in the area.

Only when one realizes the horror that the knowledge of the extent of the crimes committed in their own country produced in

---

[5] San José communiqué, *op. cit.*

the consciences of the majority of Argentinians, can one understand the profound feeling of solidarity that country feels today towards Central America, where the evil techniques of extermination were exported. Argentina is an extreme case because its involvement was real, but the desire to help, the desire to participate in the struggle for peace, to do everything possible to avoid something worse, and above all to make every effort to avoid the transfer of the East-West confrontation to the Western Hemisphere, is evident in many other Latin American countries today, such as Bolivia or Peru, and undoubtedly will be equally so in Uruguay tomorrow. One cannot isolate Central America from its Latin American context.

Last, it is worth speculating whether the Soviet Union desires an American intervention in Central America. It is obvious that Cuba does not. But, considering the extent to which Cuba is outflanked by the extreme left in the Nicaraguan regime and by a segment of the Salvadoran guerrillas, the margins within which it can act to avoid intervention are very narrow. As long as negotiatons are not expanded to include Cuba (and Contadora has always avoided bringing it into the dialogue), the only policy open to Castro's regime is the not very constructive one of raising the cost of intervention by supplying the guerrillas, and elevating Nicaragua's defense capabilities, as well as its own.

In this connection, I am convinced—though this is a different subject altogether—that today more than ever before there is a basis for meaningful negotiations between the United States and Cuba. The tranquility of a second Reagan term ought to permit such a daring initiative since only through negotiations will it be possible gradually to reintegrate Cuba into Latin America, that is, into the Western world.

III. Spain and Central America

Within a framework where tensions are growing and the Central American conflict is viewed as part of the global East-West conflict, Europe has no choice but to subordinate its policies to American interests or to move toward a confrontation with the United States, which everyone wants to avoid.

But if it proves possible to convince the United States to see the conflict in all its local and regional complexity and to strengthen the peace process, Europe can play a very broad and constructive role. Not only would this reinforce relations between Europe and Latin America, but it could make a positive and important contribution to general stability as well.

Everything I have tried to explain about the need to strengthen ties between Europe and Central America, which could (in my opinion and in that of many European politicians and academics, contribute to the stability of the Western world) has an obvious "Spanish reading." On the one hand, everything just argued is valid for Spain, which is above all a European country about to come into full EEC membership. On the other hand, some additional factors affect Spanish-Central American relations that are either absent or far less important when viewed from a purely European perspective.

It seems obvious that Spain is the European country spiritually closest to Central America. And neither from a pragmatic nor from a doctrinal perspective can this type of "closeness" be dismissed, even though it is difficult to determine its factual meaning or to measure its relevance. How can we measure in political terms, for example, the impact of Prime Minister González' popularity in Central America? How can we evaluate the fact that perhaps more than half of all the priests who work in Central America are Spanish? How relevant is the fact that the first meeting of the Contadora ministers outside of the region took place in Madrid in October 1984.

Those are, of course, unanswerable questions, but they do suggest some undeniable realities. For example, one can say that events in Central America in general have a greater impact on public opinion in Spain than in other European countries. Hence, the sensitivity of Spanish political leaders to the present crisis is also greater. It can also be said that what happens in Spain is more closely followed in Central America and better known than what happens in other European countries. In particular, the Central American countries, just as the rest of Latin America, have followed the political transition in Spain with considerable intensity.

The Impact of the Political Transition in Spain (1975–1985) on Central America

Spain is probably the only country in the world that in recent times has passed from dictatorship[6] to democracy without having lost an external war, without having had a sponsor country supervise the transition, and without having had to suppress a revolution en route. (These appear to be the three classic ways of moving to liberal democracy.) This achievement, which is the first real reason for national pride that the Spanish people have had in centuries and which has not been sufficiently appreciated by foreign observers, has had undeniably important repercussions throughout Latin America.

For the first time in many years, the Spanish-speaking American countries, which are characterized by their ethnic and cultural diversity, have shown an interest in reclaiming the Hispanic elements of their own identity. As King Juan Carlos put it in his commencement address at Harvard University in June 1984, "Spain is no longer seen as the symbol of a difficult past, but as that of a better future."

This reversal in the way the Hispanic heritage is perceived in Latin America is important not so much in itself, nor because of the possibilities of exporting the Spanish political "model." The latter is nil, because any model that is not based on the specific realities to which it is going to be applied is doomed to failure. What has happened in Spain is not a model, but it is a source of inspiration and hope. It is even more important because of the time at which it has occurred, when the collective frustration of Latin America seems to have reached a historical zenith. The two most clear manifestations of that frustration are the Central American crisis and the debt problem. Both touch on basic concepts of sovereignty and national independence.

In this situation, the search for "signs of an identity" that are essentially Latin American and that promote integration becomes paramount. Even though the economic crisis has destroyed or

---

[6] I am referring, of course, to lengthy institutionalized dictatorships, and not to brief military "episodes" that do not destroy structures or preexisting political traditions.

weakened most efforts at economic and political integration, the awareness that such integration is desirable, necessary and un-avoidable grows more intense every day. In fact, these very crises are, paradoxically, forcing moves toward the collective responses that are an expression of this need (for example, meetings of the debtor countries, the Contadora Group, etc.).

In Central America where, as we have seen, the problems of national identity are so interwoven with the general conflict that they have become an inseparable aspect of that conflict, any source of identity that is rational, non-polemical, and not defined in terms of some real or imagined enemy is a positive step. It is here that the changing symbolism of the region's Hispanic roots enters the picture.

There are other less abstract areas in which democratization in Spain has influenced Central America. These include the increasing political contacts at all levels, not just governmental. Insofar as these have expanded to the left of the political spectrum, they are particularly significant. For many years the Latin American left was locked in generic Third World revolutionary self-consciousness as the "damnés de la terre," colored in Central America by Castroism and anti-Americanism and very isolated from the West. In this sense, the political legitimization of Spanish socialism has served in some measure as a catalyst for the Latin American left's opening to more western-style definitions. The importance of the Spanish Socialist Workers' Party in this process, both before and after its assumption of power, is widely recognized.

Another feature of the transition is the Spanish King, who has become a regular visitor to Latin America. In 1976 he announced his intention of visiting each and every country of the Hemisphere. He has since made more than a dozen trips and has visited some Latin American countries twice because they have repeatedly invited him either to commemorate historic anniversaries or to celebrate the return to democracy in countries, like Argentina, where he had made difficult trips during dictatorial regimes.[7]

The King's travels are important on the one hand for their con-

---

[7] Today the only countries he has not visited besides Bolivia (where he has scheduled a trip for the spring of 1985) are Chile, Cuba, Nicaragua and Paraguay.

tribution to the feeling of community that is gaining momentum in Spanish America, and on the other in ways that are difficult to summarize because of their complex meaning. It is somewhat similar to what is happening with his own role in Spain today, which has become infinitely more important than what one would deduce from examining his constitutional duties. Though an exotic element in Latin America and a symbol of a distant pre-independence past, nevertheless, because of a surprising combination of factors that includes his own personality, the message of democracy and liberty his figure symbolizes, and the needs of the countries he visits, no one has questioned such things as the King's right in July 1983 to receive the first Simón Bolivar Prize, created by UNESCO in honor of "the Liberator's" Bicentennial. Similarly in 1978 he dared to tell then-Argentinian President Jorge Rafael Videla in public that reasons of state do not justify the violation of human rights, and in April 1983 he played a leading part in the first great popular demonstration for democracy on the streets of Montevideo. Central America is present in almost all of his public speeches, as is most everything of interest to Spaniards.

The case of Prime Minister González is quite different, although equally surprising for those who try to analyze the world exclusively in power terms. When Latin American leaders meet, González is often there. He joins their meetings, reflects with them on the problems of Latin and Central America and finally signs their documents.[8] González' role with respect to Central America has varied, but his attention has always been there, before and after reaching power. He has undoubtedly been instrumental in opening up the Socialist International's sensibility to Central American problems and now works daily—as we all do in the Spanish Administration—to raise the level of European awareness of this problem in government circles.

The Spanish political process has also affected the European perception of the crisis in Central America quite considerably. In one of the many seminars that have taken place in Spain to discuss

---

[8] Caracas Declaration of February 3, 1984, signed by Alfonsín of Argentina, Betancur of Colombia, Siles Zuazo of Bolivia, Ortega of Nicaragua, Lusinchi of Venezuela, Monge of Costa Rica, Blanco of the Dominican Republic, de la Espriella of Panama and, González.

the situation in Cental America, a Central European speaker emphasized the importance of democratization on the Iberian peninsula because, in his words, "to understand the problems of a given region the colonizer's interpretation is absolutely necessary." The colonizer has always been there, but its opinion interested no one until the internal political changes legitimated its views.

All this could lead to the conclusion that Spain has such close and privileged relations with the countries of Central America and such a potential for influence in the region that it could itself become another element in the situation, and particularly in the growing linkage with Europe. I do not think, however, that this would be totally accurate.

Spain's Relations with Central America

Spain has good relations with most of the Central American countries although there is ample room for improvement in all fields.[9] In particular, our economic links and aid programs leave much to be desired. Until a decade ago, Spain was an aid-recipient country, so our present levels of development assistance and capital export are still modest. The growing needs of Central American economies make it difficult to expand trade and exchanges without a decisive aid component. Last year for the first time Spain launched an integral technical cooperation program with three countries— Costa Rica, Nicaragua and Honduras—that goes beyond the small isolated projects in which Spain had been involved up to now. Spain is trying to open the way to more dynamic forms of cooperation in which its youth can actively participate. Still, the total value of the project is modest. Spain's cultural presence is, of course, important but it is largely spontaneous. Private investment rose sharply in the 1960s and 1970s but is now in retreat because of the slump.

Nevertheless, I do not believe that Spain's lack of significant economic weight is a serious a problem, as is sometimes suggested. The great powers exercise influence by giving massive aid

---

[9] It has recently renewed relations with Guatemala, which were broken after the burning of the Spanish Embassy in 1980.

to governments or opposition movements, but not having strong links of this kind can give middle-sized countries greater freedom of action, especially in a context as changing and fluid as that of Central America. It allows for the establishment of non-dominating, more egalitarian relationships that have value in themselves.

On the political level, what characterizes Spain's relations with Central America is not that they are particularly intense, but that over the last years the Spanish have been able to develop a capacity for dialogue with almost all the actors in the conflict. Spain has always avoided both dogmatic oversimplification and shortsighted pragmatism in its government analyses and actions. It has sought not only to use the same language with all active participants in the region, but also to include that language within the general guidelines of its foreign policy and ideological definition.

This has been possible, not because Spain is more inclined to policy coherence than other governments are, but because for Spain, and for its foreign and domestic policy as a whole, Central America is not some distant appendage. Rather it is a region to which Spaniards feel very close and where reckless and heady policies must be avoided. Any such adventure would have immediate repercussions on Spain's domestic tranquility. As Prime Minister González often notes, Spain is not one of those governments that likes revolutions so long as they occur elsewhere.

In such circumstances, drawing fine lines is unavoidable, and, consequently so is the danger of not satisfying anyone. Those who have closely followed Spain's positions and its day-to-day policies toward the crisis in Central America over the last two years— which will not be repeated or justified here because that is not the theme of this essay—will understand this clearly.

In exchange for that risk, Spain has also reaped some benefits. The Central Americans have come to understand very well that Spain's attitudes and positions are not designed to improve its image in other regions of the world or to illustrate its independence on "secondary" issues so that it will look better when it accepts discipline on essentials. If it is true that no party to the Central American conflict sees an unconditional ally in Spain, then almost all accept Spain as a friend because, as is sometimes said, friendship is a question of taking someone absolutely seriously. At this time, this absolute seriousness means, in the Spanish view, accepting that the search for a positive solution to the present crisis in Central America cannot be subordinated to the global interests of the East-West confrontation.

Central America in Spanish Politics

Any observer of Spain can perceive the emotional importance that the Central American issue has in Spanish politics. A current of sympathy for the peoples of Latin America, who are regarded as a part of the family of Hispanic nations, runs throughout Spanish society and creates links of primary solidarity, probably no less strong than those felt by the different communities of the Arab world or among Jews in the United States, Israel and the Soviet Union.

Still in the Central American case there are a few specific aspects that should be emphasized. Independence in Central America was obtained mainly as a by-product of the Mexican struggle to the north and the Bolivarian liberation to the south. There was not much fighting. But the Spanish perception of the entire Central American problem is colored by what is the most significant historical event for twentieth-century Spain, which left its imprint on all contemporary Spanish culture and politics: the Cuban War or, as it is known in the United States, the "Spanish-American War." In 1898 the United States put an end to any remaining Spanish influence in the Hemisphere and laid the basis for its own hegemony. The feeling that Cubans and Spaniards were defeated together rapidly took root in Spain, which withdrew into itelf as it entered a long period of isolation. In the four decades that followed, Spain's only triumph in any field was a most profound cultural flowering in which, for the first time since Latin America's independence, the literary and artistic vanguards on both sides of the ocean reencountered each other. The Nicaraguan poet Rubén Darío is the symbol of that reunion, which has been uninterrupted ever since.

This is important both with respect to Spain's general feeling of solidarity with Central America and with respect to the specific political positions of the Spanish government (for example, its rejection of such suggestions as sending mine sweepers to clear the Nicaraguan coasts). It marks the limits of solidarity beyond which no Spaniard would want to overstep.

Aside from this, naturally there are different perceptions of the problem in Spain according to individuals' differing positions on the political spectrum. The right, today in opposition, is evidently more sensitive to the global analyses that it tries hard to share. It warns about the danger of "communist aggression" in El Salvador and harshly criticizes the Sandinista regime and the Spanish government for supporting it. But even those efforts have their limits, and the rejection of the Kissinger Commission report, for example, was almost as strong on the Spanish right as on the left, although obviously for different reasons. The feeling of solidarity with Central Americans can thus take on different colors, but it is very widespread.

Let me in conclusion address two aspects of Spanish policy that are critical and that could be deeply influenced, although in very different ways, by events in Central America: the first is the issue of NATO, the other is Spain's joining in the European Economic Community.

If the Central American situation deteriorates still further, and particularly if the dream of a military solution to the crisis leads to a massive U.S. military intervention, whether in El Salvador to support a legitimate government or in Nicaragua against the Sandinista regime, the impact on Spanish public opinion will be very great. It could substantially alter the basis on which Spain is formulating a solution to the problem of its specific Alliance engagement and its contribution to the defense of the West. As I indicated above, a major U.S. military intervention could jeopardize the continued membership of Spain in NATO.

It might be of interest to point out that one does not find in Spain the ingrained anti-American reflex that is sometimes found in other European countries that underwent postwar occupation. But the opposite reflex, that of a vision of liberation by America, a vision based on the experience of the two wars in which Spain did not participate, is also absent. That is why the Spanish situation is so special. There is a strong historical, neutralist tradition, and perhaps some drops of latent anti-Americanism that can be traced to 1953 when the United States signed agreements with Franco giving Spain economic assistance in exchange for the establishment of four U.S. military bases on Spanish soil. Spain, with no freedom of expression and with its jails full of dissidents, was for many years "a bulwark of the West." This is the reason why many Spaniards shivered when on February 23, 1981, after being asked what position the American government would take if the coup d'état were to succeed, then-Secretary of State Alexander Haig replied offhandedly that he had no comments to make on "internal matters." The lack of concern for democratic institutions that this statement seemed to reflect could presumably apply to Central America as well. That is one reason why the entire issue of Central America is so important to Spain today.

With respect to the EEC, Spain's approaching integration into the Common Market is seen with suspicion by some Latin American countries that fear Spain will cut its ties to them and renounce the special relationship that all are engaged in building. After all, for some time before Franco's death, when Spain's entry into the EEC seemed impossible, the idea of renouncing European integration and substituting for it a stronger economic connection with Latin America was considered. But the differing levels of economic development and the problems derived from distance never made this feasible. Most Latin American countries now understand and support Spain's EEC membership, and it is obvious that Spain would not consider joining the EEC if it did not provide across-the-board benefits to Latin America. For that reason, Spain sees the European-Latin American connection recently inaugurated in Costa Rica as only the first step toward developing a more profound relationship between the two regions and the beginning of a new balance in the EEC's foreign policy toward the less developed areas of the world.

In sum, Spain has neither the means nor, what is more important, the ambition to exercise real power in the Central American crisis. But Spain's special links to the countries involved, its status as an ally of the United States, its forthcoming entry into the European Economic Community, and the fact that it has always maintained good relations with Cuba confer on it a considerable capacity for dialogue that could have some value. Spain has never sought a role as a mediator, but it cannot avoid its responsibility to support or forward any initiative that may improve the situation. For the time being Spaniards consider it their obligation to offer support that is more than rhetorical and that reinforces, from many different angles, the effort hitherto carried on by the Contadora countries to find a negotiated regional solution.

Irving Kristol

Should Europe Be Concerned About Central America?

American policy toward Central America is certainly an important and perplexing issue for the United States. It is also clearly an issue of overriding importance for the nations of Central America and of Latin America as a whole. But why is it an issue for the nations of Western Europe? To an American the answer to that question is not at all self-evident. Yet it is a fact, obvious to even the most casual observer, that the triangular relations among the United States, Central and Latin America, and Western Europe do constitute an issue of concern and controversy to everyone involved. How can this be explained? Is it a relatively superficial and trivial dispute over tactics, where dissension is only a fragment of a larger consensus? Or does it perhaps raise some fundamental questions about diverging visions of world politics—of the nature of world disorder and of the kind of possible order that one might strive for—that are increasingly separating the United States from its West European allies?

From the standpoint of traditional *Realpolitik*, and its rigorous conception of national self-interest, there seems little economic or strategic reason for Western Europe to have any kind of Central American policy—especially one that brings it into conflict with its major ally, the United States. True, Spain does have, or claims to have, historic and cultural connections with the Spanish-speaking nations south of the U.S. border, but if it were only Spain that were involved, the Western Alliance would not be much troubled. The North Atlantic Treaty Organization, after all, managed quite well for many years without Spain as a member, and if Spanish discontent with American policy caused it to leave NATO, it would provoke something less than a crisis.[1] Spain is not a tradi-

---

[1] *Editor's Note:* A national referendum on Spain's continuation in NATO is to take place by the spring of 1986.

tional ally of the United States, as is Great Britain or France, and, unlike West Germany, its military contribution to NATO is not essential to NATO's survival. Besides, there are some grounds for wondering whether those "close cultural ties" between Spain and Hispanic America are as substantial as is sometimes asserted, and if they are not more a rationale for criticism of American foreign policy than a reason for it.

Whatever the situation with respect to Spain, however, the case of Great Britain, France or West Germany seems unambiguous. Again, from the standpoint of *Realpolitik*, their criticisms—often overt and provocative—of American foreign policy in Central America are difficult to make sense of. Neither economically nor strategically can that area be of much interest to them. One can appreciate their fears that, as a result of its pursuing an erroneous policy in Central America, the United States will be distracted from its more important—in their eyes, much more important— commitments, such as the defense of Western Europe. One would understand, therefore, if these nations privately communicated to the State Department their strong displeasure and keen apprehension about the course of this policy. Nor would it be surprising if such communications found their way into the media, as such private communications have a way of doing, but our West European allies go much further than this. They express open and official dissatisfaction with American policy—even take official actions that are clear signs of sympathy with those in Central America who are engaged in activities hostile to the United States, at least as the United States perceives and interprets those activities. Surely our European allies cannot believe that such behavior will strengthen the Western Alliance.

Under some circumstances it may become necessary for the United States to intervene militarily in Central America. Should such an intervention occur, what will our West European allies say and do? *That* will be the critical moment for the Western Alliance as the very existence of NATO itself may be at stake. If our allies are not ready to support us when we are in trouble, it is highly improbable that the American people will see much point in supporting them when they are in trouble. This does not mean that the United States will become indifferent to the fate of Western Europe. That is unthinkable, but it is not impossible to conceive of an American military policy toward Western Europe that, while resistant to Soviet aggression, is not so dependent on Western European wishes and concerns.

Some might make the legalistic argument that the Western Alliance, as defined by NATO's charter, has specified geographical limits—limits coterminous with the interests of Western Europe, as defined by Western Europe. This is indeed literally the case, and it is equally the case that Central America is not within those limits. But it is hard to take this legalistic response too seriously. Certainly, the idea behind the establishment of NATO was not that the United States and Western Europe would agree on terms for the defense of Western Europe and would agree to disagree when policies vis-à-vis Latin America, the Middle East, or Asia diverged. Had such an idea been candidly expressed at the time, NATO might well have died aborning. Such legalisms are not the stuff of which enduring alliances are made. The assumption behind NATO was, not only that the United States and the nations of Western Europe would act in concert so as to defend Western Europe, but also that the foreign policies of these allied nations would be "coordinated" so that, whenever disagreements occurred over other areas of the world, a spirit of solidarity would nevertheless prevail.

This was a general assumption in both European and U.S. circles. In addition, however, there was a further, tacit American assumption that, since the United States was the largest and most powerful member of the Alliance and had made the most extraordinary commitment—to risk its national existence in order to defend other nations' territorial integrity—the nations of Western Europe would naturally be deferential toward American policy in such a non-NATO area as the Western Hemisphere. The American people have always interpreted the NATO Alliance in this light, and one cannot imagine their making such a dangerous commitment without such an assumption being made.

Was it, is it, a presumptuous assumption? In any alliance the vote of the most powerful member always carries extraordinary, and usually decisive, weight. One takes this for granted. For all one knows, some of America's other allies—Israel, South Korea, Taiwan, Turkey—are also unhappy with U.S. Central America policy. If so, they avoid any public, official expression of such unhappiness, since they would see it as a gratuitous affront to a crucial ally. The nations of Western Europe, of course, are not so utterly dependent on the United States for their survival. Even so, one would expect them to exercise more discretion in word and deed when it came to Central America. Apparently they either do not feel the need to do so or else feel the need not to do so.

The latter seems more plausible. When one speaks to friendly West Europeans about this matter, one is provided with the reassurance that much of this public behavior is "merely" a response to the demands of domestic politics. This is doubtless the case. However, behind that word "merely" there lies a hinterland of meanings that cannot be so easily dismissed. What is it about domestic politics in the nations of Western Europe that coerces their governments—even nominally conservative governments, and unquestionably pro-American governments—to act in so disruptive a way? And what does this signify for the Western Alliance as a whole?

The Divergence in Political Ethos

A nation's foreign policy—and most especially a democracy's foreign policy—is always responsive to considerations of domestic politics. Indeed, in an era of ideological politics, which ours is, foreign policy tends to be a continuation of domestic policy by other means. All diplomats and foreign policy professionals know this and deplore it. They would prefer to see foreign policy insulated as much as possible from what they call "the vagaries" of domestic policy. But professionals in foreign policy are probably the last people in the world one would wish to consult if one wanted to understand the fundamental, shaping realities of world politics today. Such professionals tend to be blind to the way in which foreign policy is linked to the political ethos of a nation. It is only a bit of an exaggeration to say that foreign policy professionals usually find they have more in common with other foreign policy professionals than with the citizenry of their own countries.

The basic reason for the increasing tensions between the United States and its West European allies—and not only in the case of Central America, which is more symptom than cause—is the divergence that has occurred, ever since World War II, in the political ethos of the United States and Western Europe. This divergence can be simply stated: the political ethos of Western Europe has been significantly influenced by socialist ideas and socialist modes of thinking, while the political ethos of the United States has been only superficially affected by them.

It will be said that the term "political ethos" is too imprecise to explain anything. Well, imprecise it is, but meaningless it is not. All institutions—armies, universities, political parties, churches—develop an ethos that suffuses the institution in an osmosis-like way. An ethos consists of a set of shared values—as to both ends and means—that are passed on from one generation to another, usually in a somewhat modified, but nevertheless recognizable, form. The American political ethos today is not radically different from what it was 75 years ago. There have been great changes in American society, of course, but the political ethos has adapted itself to these changes—has, it can even be said, co-opted these changes—while preserving its essential features. The average American's conception of the "good life" is continuous with that of his grandparents, as is his conviction that the "American way of life" is universally desirable, even if not universally attainable.

In all of these respects, Western Europe has become different from the United States—and from what it once was. Opinion polls reveal this difference dramatically. They show the American people to be far more patriotic than the peoples of Western Europe. Actually, the polls' use of the term "patriotic" is questionable. They did not probe *love* of country, which is surely as strong in Western Europe as in the United States. What they did probe was *pride* in country—an emotion that is more allied to what one used to call "nationalism" than to "patriotism," narrowly defined. The term nationalism is not, these days, in good odor and is gingerly avoided. But a shift in vocabulary, though it always tells us something, does not always accurately reflect a corresponding change in reality. It may even reflect nothing more than an unsuccessful effort to evade this reality. And the plain fact is that today the spirit of nationalism is very strong and active in the United States, while it is relatively quiescent in Western Europe. It is quiescent because it has been overlaid and stifled by another spirit, arising out of the

ethos of socialism—or, to be more precise, European social democracy, which is the socialist ethos struggling to find expression
within the confines of liberal, representative democracy.

One often hears it said that it is perfectly *natural* for Western
Europe to have a different world view from that of the United
States, since the nations of Western Europe, not defining themselves as world powers, are *naturally* inclined to put parochial-
geographical considerations first and to avoid any involvement in
distant areas. But just how "natural" is this? Are the nations of
Western Europe, with a combined population equal to that of the
Soviet Union and with far healthier economies, really all that
weak? Even taken individually, are Great Britain, France, or West
Germany so weak that each could not play a more active role in
world affairs if it so wished? Are these nations simply nothing
more than magnified versions of Sweden or Holland? Well, they
are if they think they are, and they will think they are if they
believe it is right for them and good for the world to be that way.

And that is the way they will think to the degree that the socialist impulse—at least in its Western, social-democratic version—
predominates over the nationalist impulse. One has to qualify the
proposition in this way because non-Western versions of socialism
are easily compatible with nationalism. This is because those
countries in the "Third World" that claim to be socialist have, in
truth, political and economic systems that are an ad hoc mélange
of Soviet-style communism, Italian-style fascism, and indigenous,
traditional authoritarianism. And, of course, authentically communist countries are firmly nationalistic, since nationalism is what
they fall back on when their Marxist-Leninist ideology becomes a
petrified doctrine with little popular appeal. It is only in those
nations where the European version of social democracy has had a
profound influence on political thinking—not only of socialists,
but of everyone—that one finds the nationalist impulse in a state
of malnutrition.

Socialist doctrine, however belligerent with regard to domestic
policy, has always had a strong pacifist component when it came
to foreign policy. Just as proponents of capitalism prior to World
War I argued that the spread of the commercial spirit and commercial institutions throughout the world would work to prevent

future wars, so do socialists believe that the spread of the socialist spirit and socialist institutions throughout the world will make national conflicts but a bad memory. In both cases, a dogmatic economic determinism replaces a knowledge of history, political philosophy, and human nature. It is no accident, to borrow a Marxist phrase, that there is no socialist literature on foreign policy. To the degree that socialism becomes a reality in the world, foreign policy becomes theoretically otiose.

This point of view, in its various hues, is extremely powerful in Western Europe. While it exists in the United States too—that portion of the political spectrum which Americans call "liberalism" shades into a milder version of European social democracy— it is relatively weak. The common European perception of the United States as a "capitalist" nation, in a sense that no European nation—not even Margaret Thatcher's Britain—can (or does) claim to be, is not incorrect. The United States, to be sure, has its welfare state, just as do the West Europeans. However, where the national psychology of Western Europe has been much affected by the welfare state, the national psychology of the United States, in the absence of a socialist movement, has been surprisingly little influenced by it. The bourgeois-capitalist spirit does in fact exist in Western Europe, but there it does not possess the status of a popular orthodoxy, both intellectual and moral, that it does in the United States.

The foreign policy of Western Europe, to the degree that it has been responsive to the socialist mode of thought, has therefore been defensive and parochial. Having little instinctive confidence in the righteous use of national power, and assuming that the world's future will be shaped more by "economic forces" than by purposive national action, its posture is defensive. "Watchful waiting" would be a fair description.

There are two other ways in which the socialist cast of mind caused Western Europe to recoil from a more assertive foreign policy. The first has to do with its imperial past, about which most Europeans are convinced they ought to feel guilty. As a result they are inhibited from taking any action that might even seem to be "imperialistic." It is impossible for any sense of national pride to flourish if this simple-minded view of European imperialism continues to prevail. Actually, there is no lack of evidence for a revisionist view of European imperialsm, and perhaps one will eventually emerge. But as yet there are no signs of it.

Second, because European socialism and European communism have a common root in Marxism, European socialists are at least partially disarmed ideologically when confronting militant communists. They even find it difficult to repudiate without reservation the Leninist version of Marxism which is now communist dogma (and have never in fact done so). To do so would be to commit themselves to a "pure," pragmatic kind of social democracy, as proposed by Edouard Bernstein early in this century. And the trouble with this version of social democracy is that, while it may well be consistent with democracy, it doesn't appear to be bringing socialism closer to becoming a reality.

Social democratic parties in Europe are "movements," not merely political parties in the bourgeois-parliamentary sense. Their mission is to create a new social order, based on a new way of life, not merely to govern well. So their dilemma can be summed up as follows: European social democracy can govern democratically, but it cannot move the nation to socialism; should it try to institute "true socialism," it would have to dissociate itself from bourgeois, parliamentary democracy, with its free, frequent elections, and move at least part way along the path designed by Marxist-Leninism. Unwilling to do either, it expends its energy in halfheartedly undermining capitalism and in halfheartedly opposing communism. Meanwhile, the polity as a whole has no clear ideological self-definition by which to take its bearings in a worldwide ideological conflict.

And it *is* a worldwide ideological conflict. This is not a fact that diplomats and foreign-service professionals can easily accept, since it falls outside the category of "international relations" as their tradition, and all of our textbooks, define it. Indeed, most professionals in the field of foreign affairs work very hard at trying to persuade everyone that, to the degree that ideological conflict is a force in the world today, it is all a serious error—one that should be corrected by substituting for ideological passions the cooler considerations that ought to prevail if "international relations" were to be what they used to be in the nineteenth century.

Unfortunately, the world is what it is, not what it used to be or ought to be. The twentieth century breeds secular, political religions—fascism, communism, or some mixture of the two—all of which have as their goal the destruction of bourgeois-capitalist-parliamentary democracy. The origins of this impulse lie back in the nineteenth century, and the socialist idea itself, whether in its "utopian" or "scientific-Marxist" forms, is one of its seedbeds. It is not the only one, of course. "Anti-capitalism" of the political right was, prior to World War II, and especially prior to World War I, also much in evidence. Basically, all such "movements"—a term which is itself borrowed from the history of religion—are reactions against the political philosophy of liberal individualism and aim to restore a "political community" in which the interests of the individual are completely identified with, and therefore ruthlessly subordinated to, the "public interest" as defined by a ruling elite. For most of human history people have lived in such "political communities," and prior to the eighteenth century it was thought to be the only moral type of political association. So it is surely an error to regard these movements as transient political pathologies, to be "treated" and "cured" as if they represented cases of hysterical neurosis. They are—at least so far as one can see into the future—real alternatives to democratic capitalism and a constant challenge to its survival.

The response to this challenge has been very different in the United States and in Western Europe. The nations of Western Europe have, over the years, lost their enthusiasm for the political philosophy of liberal individualism and the economic, social and political institutions derived from that philosophy. In their daily life, they may remain attached to those institutions on the whole and prefer them to proposed alternatives, but it is a kind of loveless marriage. They reject the claim of Marxist-Leninism to own the future but propose no claim of their own as to such ownership. After two disastrous European wars they are weary of anything resembling militancy. They find it convenient to think that the inherent flaws in the communist claim—above all, the obvious fact that collectivist economies are far less productive than capitalist or quasi-capitalist ones—will cause those regimes gradually to modify their hostility to the West and to move along the lines of "convergence" with Western systems.

The United States, in contrast, is still enthusiastically loyal to the philosophy of liberal individualism—indeed, has become increasingly enthusiastic in recent years. That is the meaning of the much-publicized and very real "conservative" trend in American politics. The people of the United States still believe that they own the future—that their economic-social-political system, their way of life, is still a viable and inherently desirable alternative for all other nations.

Presumptuous and naive this vision may be, but few can doubt that it is deeply rooted in the hearts and minds of the American people. Moreover, this American self-confidence is rooted in fact—in the fact that the American economic system does work so as to attach to itself the loyalties of its citizens, and that such loyalties are attached to the American political system even more strongly, with a kind of quasi-religious intensity. If it works in the United States, a nation of immigrants, why not elsewhere? Why not everywhere? Not instantly, to be sure. But why not eventually?

Ideologies in Conflict

This American self-confidence has an important and frequently overlooked implication for American foreign policy. To the world, the American attitude and most specifically the foreign policy of the United States, is imbued with a missionary spirit that makes history-weary Europeans uncomfortable. It is not, as some critics claim, a crusading spirit and does not, except in major wars, yield a crusading foreign policy. The American people believe that time is on their side. This is the historic rationale for American isolationism, which emphasized the power of the American example and which never for a moment assumed that the survival of the United States would occur in a permanently hostile world. It also explains the easy acceptance of the idea of "containment" of the Soviet Union, or even Cuba. So long as "time" (i.e., history as progress) is given the chance to bear its natural fruits, the American people are not particularly distressed by the coming into existence of communist or anti-democratic regimes here or there. The trouble, as they see it, is that communist regimes are always then intervening to abort the fruits of time. It is this problem, they feel, that American foreign policy must candidly confront.

The Soviet Union, of course, also believes officially that history is on its side—though its notion of history is of the nineteenth-century, militant, Hegelian-Marxist variety, as against the more easy-going eighteenth-century idea of progress. In between these two "political myths," as a sociologist would call them, lies the French Revolution, with its messianic promise of a "revolution" that would solve, simultaneously, all economic, political and social problems. When one hears it said that the United States must "adapt" to "revolutionary change" in the world, it is the appeasement of such political messianism that is meant. The American Revolution, in contrast, promised only individual liberty within a structure of popular government. It did not promise to abolish poverty; it left that task to the workings of a commercial society and to a process of economic growth as envisioned by Adam Smith. Nor did it promise to abolish social and economic (as distinct from legal) inequalities—an issue that it assumed economic growth would assuage but that never could be made to vanish, humanity being what it is.

The kind of political messianism incarnated in the Soviet and other communist regimes is not only "crusading" in principle, but, in recent decades it has been moved to a kind of desperation in its militancy. All expectations that the Soviet regime would mellow with time have been disappointed. The reason is twofold. First, the kind of collectivist economic system proposed by Marxism simply does not work in a modern, industrial, technological society. Second, the political system constructed according to the Leninist prescription does not work either, in the sense that it can never secure popular consent. For a communist regime to "mellow" in any substantial way it would have to disassociate itself from the political messianism that is the very basis of its legitimacy. The only way it can affirm that legitimacy is in the area of foreign affairs, where it might bully the world into believing that it does in truth represent the "wave of the future." To the degree it can succeed in such an endeavor, it can also bully its own population into resigning itself to the seemingly inevitable.

So world politics today revolves around this ideological clash between two great powers, the Soviet Union and the United States. In this clash, the Soviet ideology is active, the American ideology reactive—but the ideologies are what are in conflict, not "national interests" in the more conventional sense of the term, and not "national security" in any purely strategic sense of the term. A great many scholars have expended much ingenuity in trying to demonstrate that Soviet foreign policy is really nothing more than traditional Russian foreign policy in modern dress. Obviously, since the Soviet regime occupies the Russian nation, there is bound to be some overlap. But can any one imagine a tsar establishing a colony or a protectorate in Cuba, or in Nicaragua? No conception of "great power politics" can make sense of such an action, while the ideological impulse behind Soviet foreign policy—a self-proclaimed ideological impulse—explains it all too easily.

Those Europeans who insist that Soviet foreign policy derives from a deep sense of insecurity are correct—though in a way they cannot accept. The insecurity of the Soviet regime has little to do with the national history of the Russian people, or with any "paranoid" fears that are supposedly prompted by that history. It is rather an insecurity that flows from the radical failure of Marxist-Leninist ideology to accomplish its historic mission. It is a failed ideology that nevertheless serves as the rock on which a "church militant" has been built. The more acute and obvious the failure, the more militant the church will feel compelled to become. Efforts to appease this militancy, in the hope of softening it, are beside the point. The Soviet regime is as much a prisoner of the totalitarian system it has created as are the Soviet people.

In this conflict of ideologies, the United States is at a great disadvantage. A reactive foreign policy is always at a disadvantage when confronted with an active one, just as a reactive military policy is similarly at a disadvantage.

In addition, the messianic myth of Marxist-Leninism has an enormous appeal to the elites—sometimes even to the populace— of the world's poorer countries. It has the appeal of providing a quick solution to an intractable problem—and, moreover, an economic, social, and political solution all in one. It is a false solution, of course—a species of ideological magic. However, it does offer the kind of solution to the question of reconciling political stability with ideological quackery that only a powerful, comprehensive tyranny can provide. And for those who compose the new ruling class—they can number as much as ten percent of the population—it also offers all the advantages normally associated with such a position.

The American and European solution to the problems confronted by the world's poor countries is far less effectual. It offers much less—and delivers still less. The European-American solution is government-to-government economic aid, with the aim of alleviating poverty, decreasing economic inequality, and stimulating economic growth. Most often it does none of these things, but rather exacerbates the endemic problems. The governments that receive this aid are more often than not corrupt, do not understand the way in which free market economics spur economic growth, do not really much like free markets in any case, and have cultural-political traditions that are inimical to productive economic activity. Above all, even though they may violently reject Marxist-Leninism, these regimes feel compelled to subscribe publicly to its crucial premise: that it is possible to "solve" a country's economic problems quickly if only government sets its mind to it.

However, it is not possible. Economic growth takes time. It is to be reckoned in generations, not years or even decades. During this time political stability is needed as well as scope for the kind of individual economic freedom that created the present level of "opulence" (to use a nice, old-fashioned word out of Adam Smith) in the West (or, as some would now have it, the North). In addition, the issue of equality of economic condition must not be permitted to arise in such a way as to frustrate the possibility of economic growth. "Equality of opportunity" is the appropriate slogan for economic growth, not "equality of condition." Once you insist that everyone improve his condition equally, you have guaranteed that no one will improve his condition at all—except, perhaps, for those fortunate enough to enjoy the spoils of government.

It is hard to think of a single poor country in the world today that will candidly subscribe to this bourgeois-capitalist philosophy, the philosophy that created the modern economies of the West, though there are a few that subscribe to it implicitly. Indeed, the West itself has been so influenced by the egalitarian ethos derived from modern social democracy that it dare not even propose it publicly. The upshot is that the foreign economic policies of the West, both European and American, provoke disillusionment and resentment instead of gratitude and contentment. Nevertheless, one hears calls for ever greater economic aid, calls issued in the name of "compassion" but born out of desperation. Whether money can buy happiness may be debatable, but on the evidence it is clear that it cannot buy self-sustaining economic growth.

The Issues in Central America

In the case of Central America, all of these issues of world politics, economic growth, and political instability confront us in an especially acute way. It is a confrontation that Western Europe would like to pretend does not exist. However, it is a confrontation that the United States cannot evade—though most of the time American policy, with its emphasis on economic aid and human rights, consists in large measure of fumbling evasions.

It is very difficult for anyone to speak candidly about Central America today, since our media-drenched rhetoric has legitimated sentimentality and sanctimony at the expense of candor. It is especially difficult for an American—rich neighbors these days watch their language when talking about the troublesome poor a few streets away. Central America (with the notable exception of Costa Rica) is inhabited by a poverty-stricken population that is regularly and systematically victimized by brutal governments. One's instinct is to demand immediate reformation, to sympathize with rebellions of the poor (or of those who claim to represent the poor), and to think little about longer term consequences. For an American government to admit helplessness vis-à-vis this situation is considered intolerable. However, helping poor, suffering people is not always as easy as it seems at first glance.

There is much to be said by way of explanation, if not justification, for the traditional popular indifference in North America to events and conditions in Latin America. It never was mere parochialism. Rather, it was engendered by a sense of bewildered helplessness before the spectacle of nations engaging, decade after decade, in self-destructive behavior. The natural sensibility of Americans withdrew into a protective shell when faced with such senselessness. There are those who claim that the United States has made its own contribution to this sorry state of affairs by its

occasional blundering intervention. There is some truth to this—
but not much. With or without American interference or involvement, these peoples behaved in ways that the average American
could not even begin to understand.

It is a fact that for over a century and a half now the nations of
Central America have demonstrated an extraordinary incapacity
for self-government. To read the history of El Salvador, for instance, is rather like reading a history of agrarian reform in nineteenth-century Spain. Much happened, in terms of revolution and
counter-revolution, reformation and counter-reformation, much
blood was spilled and much eloquence uttered—but very little
changed. It is also a fact that, whenever there were a few successive years of good economic growth—and there have been many
such episodes in El Salvador's history—a political convulsion
would summarily annul most of the nation's accomplishments.
From a North American viewpoint—one shaped by an Anglo-
American political tradition—this is incomprehensible. Religious
conflict, ethnic conflict, class conflict are all understandable (if not
easily) to Americans, but the internal conflicts within Central
American nations—and throughout Latin America as well—do not
fall neatly into any such clear-cut categories. The imperatives of a
modern economy, society and polity point in the direction of a
bourgeois and prosaic way of life in which the majority concen-
trates its attention on improving its economic condition through its
own efforts while keeping politics at a distance and regarding it
pretty much as a necessary nuisance. Central American immigrants to the United States reveal or acquire these attributes almost overnight, as it were. However, in Central America itself,
they—or at least many of them—are apparently impelled to think
and act otherwise. In that context the prosaic is regarded with
disdain, not respect, while "heroic" action or fantasies of heroic
action are dominant.

Central America thus poses a most perplexing challenge to
American foreign policy. The nations of the region are either in
turmoil or in potential turmoil. And now there is a new element—
the Soviets and Cubans are intervening in that turmoil with the
intention of establishing Marxist-Leninist regimes in the area and
throughout the Southern Hemisphere as well.

Do such regimes necessarily constitute any kind of threat to the

United States? Europeans tend to think that the American government is indulging in hysterical exaggeration when it asserts they are, and the Europeans perceive the United States as reacting in an unduly "ideological" way. Why, they ask, can the United States not live amiably with neighboring nations that have different socioeconomic systems? The answer is, of course, that the United States has little trouble doing just that. There have been left-wing and quasi-socialist regimes established in Peru, Bolivia, even in Mexico, and they have not precipitated any kind of crisis in American foreign policy. But Marxist-Leninist regimes, actively supported with military aid and economic subvention by the Soviet Union, are a new kind of challenge. These tend to be totalitarian tyrannies, not the more familiar left-wing military dictatorships or one-party, left-wing governments. With massive Soviet assistance, they are enduring tyrannies—as enduring as the Soviet tyranny itself. And they (i.e., Cuba and Nicaragua) are active Soviet allies in this Hemisphere—which is to say, they are active American enemies.

Even so, it might be said, these are small and poor countries. What kind of threat can they really pose to the United States? And is it not a form of paranoia to worry excessively about a "domino effect," with successive Latin American nations toppling over into the Soviet camp? Surely those nations will not topple so easily? And if that is our concern, why do we not work to make those nations more stable and secure, instead of engaging in confrontations with the likes of Cuba or Nicaragua?

From a purely military point of view the movement of countries such as Cuba and Nicaragua into the Soviet camp is not at all such a trivial matter. Cuba today is, after the United States, the largest and most powerful military force in the Western Hemisphere—much more powerful than Canada or Brazil for instance. It has sophisticated weapons supplied by the Soviets and well-trained soldiers who can use them. (Britain might have been able to wreak its will on Argentina, but it would be hopelessly outclassed in a conflict with Cuba if it were not to use its nuclear weapons.) In addition, Cuba has provided—and it is continuing to expand such provisions—submarine bases for the Soviet fleet and airfields where Soviet planes can land. In the strict and narrowest sense of American national security—i.e., defense of the continental homeland—Cuba is no threat. It will never invade the United States. However, should there be a Soviet-American confrontation, those Soviet bases and Cuba's own military strength—to say nothing of its strategic location in the sea-lanes—would surely count for something.

And there is another consideration. Yes, there really are dominoes out there, and they are especially there in Central America. Nicaragua was the first such domino to fall, and El Salvador is now tottering. The revolution in Nicaragua had indigenous roots, but the subsequent political evolution of that nation could not have occurred without active Cuban support, which provided the Sandinistas with the military means to establish and maintain their dictatorship. It is this same support which has given poor, underpopulated Nicaragua the most powerful military force in Central America. Similarly the insurrection in El Salvador has its indigenous roots. *All* revolutions in Central America have some indigenous roots, but the insurrection in El Salvador could not be so threatening were it not for Cuban and Nicaraguan assistance to the rebels. And if a Marxist-Leninist regime is once established in El Salvador, what will happen to Honduras, Costa Rica, Guatemala and Panama, where embryonic revolutionary movements are already active? And what, eventually, will happen to Mexico itself? These are all very shaky regimes, rife with corruption and with ineffectual military establishments. Their vulnerability is acute.

These nations are well aware of their vulnerability, which is why they are now participating in or supportive of the so-called "Contadora process." Yet, though everyone expresses pious approval of the Contadora Group's mediation efforts, the sad truth is that it is more political theater than anything else. The Contadora countries (i.e., Mexico, Venezuela, Panama and Colombia) have no independent "leverage" on the situation—they are simply too weak. And there are no "misunderstandings" to clear up, since the United States and the Sandinistas understand each other well enough and are, moreover, in constant communication with one another. So the Contadora nations cannot constitute a "third force" that would change the present realities in Central America.

It might be said that the only sensible approach to this problem is to make all of the above nations less vulnerable. Yes, certainly—but more easily said than done. It is true that our economic assistance programs could and should be reformed so as to make them more effective. Too often, these programs are constructed either by bankers or politicians or the foreign aid bureaucracy itself, with equally deleterious results. The bankers are always prescribing economy in government and austerity for the people; but economy in government means firing the bulk of those corrupt, time-serving bureaucrats who constitute the government's own popular base, and austerity is not at all something the peoples of Central America need more of. As for the politicians, they are usually eager to tie strings to American aid programs, conditioning the aid to such factors as the recipient government showing greater respect for human rights and/or democratic procedures, or giving a substantial portion of the aid directly to the poor. But these governments, whether of the left or right, rarely share the American concern for human rights and are in any case usually too weak vis-à-vis the military, or the police, or other powerful groups to do very much about it.

As for directing economic aid to the poor, this is probably the worst kind of economic assistance. It is not more generous welfare allotments that these countries need but more vigorous economic growth. In this approach the proper use of our economic aid should be to finance cuts in tax rates—taxes are absurdly high in all these countries—along with cuts in governmental subsidies to inefficient producers. These and other measures to spur private investment and private economic activity hold out the hope of putting their economies on a progressive economic track. The Reagan Administration has made some tentative moves in this direction, but the resistance is strong—both within the U.S. Congress and from the Central American governments themselves. The thinking of the latter about economics is deeply rooted in the Hispanic-Catholic cultural tradition, a paternalistic, anti-individualistic tradition to which the very idea of economic growth through the (relatively) free economic activity of the individual is alien. Central America has produced its fair share of competent economists, but practically all of them are educated in the United States and most of them never go back to their native lands.

In any case, even if a more thoughtful program of American economic aid were in place, one could not expect any remarkable effects over the short term. It is probable that the statistical results would, within a few years, be significantly positive, but macroeconomic statistics are one thing while personal economic experience is another. Indeed, they can actually work against one another. The United States is fortunate in that, up until the late 1940s, its economic development could occur without anyone having the faintest idea what its macroeconomic condition was, or even how to go about calculating the relevant statistics. Today, however, when a government announces that real gross national product grew by seven percent last year, a great many people will promptly wonder why they have not seen a piece of that action. In truth, they might not have. Economic growth at the personal level is generally a very slow and often intermittent affair. Frequently it is an intergenerational affair with parents taking their pleasure in seeing their children improve their condition. For the processes of economic growth to take full effect, what is needed is patience, faith in a free market economy, and above all the willingness of the citizenry to defer gratification. These preconditions will not exist if the political culture does not emphatically and candidly advocate them. Such a political culture may yet emerge in Latin America, but at the moment the "bourgeois ethos," which is what we are describing, lives a life apart from the political thinking that dominates that area.

This puts the United States in a quandary. Economic assistance does not really provide an answer to the immediate threat of Marxist-Leninist insurrection. Military assistance to friendly governments is obviously far more significant, but our allies in Western Europe, instead of participating in such military assistance or at the very least giving their open approval to it, have either coolly distanced themselves from it or openly expressed disapproval. A few of our NATO allies have even gone so far as to send economic aid to Nicaragua! Anyone who believes that the NATO Alliance can for long survive such discord is possessed of an overdeveloped will to believe.

Implications for the Western Alliance

The fundamental reason our European allies insist on refusing to support American policies in Central America is that they do not believe—prefer not to believe—that at the heart of world politics today is an ideological conflict between two political models of the future: some version of Marxist-Leninism on the one hand and some version of democratic capitalism on the other. Sometimes this war is "cold," sometimes it is "hot," but it is always there. The Soviet government knows it, indeed says it. The American government knows it and occasionally says it. (Its reticence reflects the U.S. State Department's traditional, and by now somewhat archaic, concern with European sensibilities.) The American people, whatever administration is in office, know it. What is called "détente" is at best a temporary agreement between the two great powers to lower the rhetorical temperature. The Soviets have never permitted this to interfere with their actual policies. The United States, having finally perceived this (after some years of self-delusion), will proceed along the same lines. In any case, those two great powers have no control over the eruptions that are occurring daily all over the globe, inside and outside of their "spheres of influence," and such developments will ruthlessly rupture any "détente" constructed by diplomats.

To some degree the European attitude is little more than a desperate hope that it can keep comfortably aloof from the turbulence of a worldwide ideological conflict. To some degree, too, it reflects a smug conviction that both the Soviet Union and the United States are young, raw, unsophisticated powers which, with time, will learn to practice the art of *raison d'état* with that skill European statesmen and commentators feel they peculiarly possess. Yet whatever the sources of the European perspective and European conduct—and there are doubtless others that can be pointed to— one thing is clear: America's European allies are fast approaching a moment of decision. The United States is not going to remain committed to the defense of Western Europe, at the risk of nuclear annihilation, if Western Europe is not equally committed to the defense of America's interests.

One of the reasons Europeans are unaware of how close they are to this moment of decision is that there is an important segment of American opinion—what is loosely called "liberal opinion"—that seems to share their view of the world. This is a minority segment; but it is not a small minority, and it is an especially influential minority, since it includes most of the media, most of academia, and a majority—if a dwindling majority—of the foreign policy establishment. Europeans have reason to think, therefore, that the current tensions within the Western Alliance will be resolved to their satisfaction once this segment of opinion, as represented by the Democratic Party, returns to national office.

There is an illusion at work here, however. It is not that such a political reversal is unthinkable in the United States in the years to come. It certainly is thinkable and, if one looks far enough ahead, is highly probable, for the two-party system is very much alive and well in the United States. The illusion consists in thinking that the dominant liberal conception of American foreign policy is nothing but a replication of European conceptions and preconception. It often looks that way; it often sounds that way; but that is not the way it really is.

For American liberal thinking about foreign policy is itself in transition—from liberal internationalism to left-wing quasi-isolationism. In this, it is following the path already marked out by British and West German social democracy. Because it is opposed to any kind of assertive foreign policy and is so horrified at the prospect of sending American troops to fight outside the borders of the United States, it is ineluctably moving to some form of isolationism. Is it reasonable to think that a government that refuses to send American troops to fight and die in Panama or Honduras is going to find it possible, even if it wished, to send those troops to fight and die in Norway or Denmark or Greece? It is also interesting to note that during the election campaign last year when Ronald Reagan was asked if he was prepared to use nuclear weapons to defend Western Europe, he promptly answered in the affirmative. Walter Mondale evaded the question. Whether any American president actually would use nuclear weapons is another matter, but Mondale's evasion unquestionably reflected the growing anti-nuclear sentiment within American liberalism. Leaving aside the issue of whether or not this sentiment has its justifications, one has to point out that without an American willingness to resort to nuclear weapons in defense of Western Europe, the present military structure of NATO is left standing on air.

It is true that, along with this anti-nuclear posture, there is an emphasis on the importance of conventional weapons. However, the conventional forces required for those weapons are very, very expensive and the liberals in the United States have made it unequivocably clear that they wish to slow down the rate of growth of the military budget so as to sustain social spending. It is reasonable to anticipate, therefore, that under any liberal administration American conventional forces will not be stronger than they are today, while our nuclear forces will be much weaker. Under these circumstances, the idea of the United States being any kind of protector of Western Europe becomes a hazy mirage. And, at some point, a liberal American government will ratify the reality by gradually withdrawing American troops from Europe—a prospect that even now American popular opinion would probably find acceptable.

At the same time as the American left is moving toward neoisolationism, the American people are moving toward a new and more assertive nationalism, to the surprise (and discomfort) of our cosmopolitan elites. In reaction to the humiliation of Vietnam, the American people today are more insistent than ever that the United States remain a great power capable of shaping the international order. They are not opposed to the NATO Alliance—so long as that alliance does not interfere with this nationalist ambition. If the American people should ever come to feel that the two commitments are incompatible, it is NATO that will go by the board, not nationalism. One wonders if the Europeans understand this. Their reaction to the American invasion of Grenada, which was so immensely popular with the American people, suggests that they do not.

It has to be said that this new nationalism itself has something of a traditional, right-wing isolationist coloration. This is true, but it is an isolationist impulse that is, for the time being anyway, quite compatible with our commitment to NATO—by now a "conservative," because anti-Soviet, commitment. It is equally true, however, that this nationalism can lead to the kind of unilateral, assertive foreign policy that will tear the Western Alliance apart. President Reagan does indeed emphasize the thesis that American power and an unambiguous willingness to use this power will have the effect of keeping us out of "foreign wars," and he has been as supportive of NATO as any American president. On the other hand, he did send troops into Grenada—without consulting the other members of NATO.

The fact is that this new American nationalism is still in the process of defining itself in a coherent way. Although it does have a powerful isolationist component, it is important to realize that, historically, American nationalist-isolationism has been primarily directed toward (even against) Europe. The United States has *never* been isolationist vis-à-vis Central America or Latin America in general. Military intervention in the Western Hemisphere, however controversial in specific instances, has never been regarded as a "foreign" entanglement. The Monroe Doctrine may be regarded as a dead letter in the State Department or at the United Nations, but it is still a valid doctrine as far as the majority of the American people are concerned. The left-wing isolationism that has emerged in recent years is at odds with this historic attitude, which means that it is not likely to evolve into a major political force but will rather suffer the same fate as the right-wing isolationism of the 1930s—isolationist toward the wrong part of the world at the wrong time.

In addition to its isolationist aspect, however, this new American nationalism does have its assertive, unilateralist aspect—representing, as it were, a return to an older pre-Wilsonian conception of American foreign policy, a Theodore Roosevelt conception of foreign policy. One way of putting it is to say that the American people have begun to wonder why, whenever the United States government is inclined to take action somewhere in the world, it finds itself entangled in a whole patchwork of entangling alliances of whose very existence most Americans were ignorant in the first place. Not only is there NATO but there is the Southeast Asia Treaty Organization, the Rio Treaty, the Anzus Pact, etc.—to say nothing of the United Nations to which the United States government has made innumerable commitments. By now there are so many such agreements and treaties that conducting American foreign policy resembles swimming in a sea of spaghetti. All of this, of course, had as its purpose the establishment of a more stable, peaceful world order under the rule of law as well as the enhancement of American security. Yet the world seems as turbulent a place as ever—nations interpret the "rule of law" to suit their interests of the moment, and American security has not visibly been improved. All of these treaties and pacts and high-flown legalistic commitments were supposed to provide tranquility, outlaw "aggression," and ensure reliable allies in a dangerous world.

But it turns out that they have done no such thing and that all of those allies feel perfectly free to behave in non-allied ways. So American popular opinion is entering a period of disillusionment with allies and of impatience with the restraints such allies exercise upon us.

Military Intervention

In this context the issue of Central America will be absolutely crucial for American-European relations. Up to now, while the American public has been willing to send economic and military aid to friendly governments south of the U.S. border, there has been little support for outright American military intervention in any of those countries. It is possible that such aid will be sufficient to subdue the various insurrections that are stimulated and supported by Cuba and the Soviet Union; but it is also possible that it will not be sufficient. The nations of Central America—of all Latin America, in truth—are not places where one can envision political stability over the longer term. So it is perfectly conceivable that in the not-too-distant future the Reagan Administration will feel it has no alternative but to intervene militarily. Once upon a time there might have been measures of "covert action" by the Central Intelligence Agency as an alternative to overt military intervention, but over the past decade liberal-dominated Congresses have decided that such covert action is immoral and have emasculated U.S. capabilities in this respect. Ironically, this increases rather than decreases the probability of direct American military involvement.

Any administration will move toward such involvement with reluctance since it will be politically divisive at home. However, remembering Grenada and taking into account resurgent American nationalism, one can reasonably predict that it will receive the support of the majority in the United States. This will especially be the case if such intervention is so massively powerful as to produce a fairly quick military victory—a fact that the Pentagon is by now well aware of.

Such a successful military intervention would not, of course, represent any kind of longer term solution to the problems of Central America. Indeed, it is hard to imagine any kind of longer term solution that does not involve some form of political association between the United States and the countries of Central America that would itself be based on a common market and a relatively free movement of people. But that is still a dream. For the moment, military intervention or non-intervention may be the real choice.

The broad mandate given to President Reagan in his reelection indicates that the American public could now well support a military intervention under certain circumstances. This could unleash a major trans-Atlantic debate. So our allies in Western Europe should start thinking seriously about Central America. As things now stand they are too inclined to be frivolous, distancing themselves publicly from American policy in order to appease anti-American political opinion at home, while at the same time offering private assurances of solidarity. It is a shortsighted tactic—as any such appeasement generally is. A major clash between the United States and Europe over Central America could soon lead to overwhelming pressures in the United States for a redefinition of its role in NATO—even to the point of the withdrawal of U.S. forces from the European continent. This prospect is something Europeans should ponder most seriously.

Michael D. Barnes

U.S. Policy in Central America: The Challenge of Revolutionary Change

From the point of view of one who has been in the middle of the controversy in the United States over U.S. policy toward Central America, to focus on Central America as an example of the problem of coping with political instability and revolutionary change in the Third World is an excellent idea. For I am convinced that at the root of the that controversy lies the broader question of how the United States—and the West—should deal with problems of Third World political instability and revolutionary change within the framework of the global balance of power—i.e., the super-power confrontation.

The Carter Administration seemed unable to make up its mind on the answer to that question. It vacillated between an emphasis on indigenous factors and an emphasis on global factors, moving toward the latter by the end of its term. The Reagan Administration's answer, however, is clear. While some government officials, especially Foreign Service officers, recognize the importance of local factors, the dominant attitude in the Reagan Administration has consistently been that Central America is a cold-war problem that can be dealt with without reference to its indigenous character: "What we are witnessing to the south is a power play by Cuba and the Soviet Union, pure and simple," President Reagan told Cuban-American leaders as recently as March 19, 1984, in a White House meeting.[1]

The Administration sees the conflict in El Salvador not as a

---

[1] See *Weekly Compilation of Presidential Documents*, March 26, 1984, Vol. 20, No. 12, p. 383.

revolution but, in the words of its February 1981 white paper, as "a textbook case of indirect armed aggression by communist powers through Cuba."[2] It is the official Administration position that El Salvador's "revolution" occurred in October 1979 when a reformist officers' coup severed the historic link between the army and the oligarchy. Those whom most people think of as the revolutionaries are in fact, according to Administration doctrine, hired gunmen acting as the agents of outside powers. With respect to Nicaragua, the Administration's position is equally clear: what it confronts there is a problem not of revolution, but of aggression.

Nor does the Administration accept the view, which is fashionable in Europe, that its policy toward Central America is somehow a test of its approach to the Third World. For the Administration there are two worlds: the free world and the communist world. Central America is part of the former; it is "ours." And the commitment that the Administration has made is to use Central America as a place to demonstrate U.S. resolve that no more parts of "our" world will be permitted to become part of "their" world. The Administration came into office pledged to reassert the hegemony that the United States had traditionally enjoyed in Central America before it was bothered with notions such as the "Third World."

This is exactly the wrong way to look at Central America. Current U.S. policy is based on a fundamental misunderstanding of what is happening in Central America. Because of this misunderstanding, U.S. policy exacerbates problems in the region and leads in the opposite direction from the one in which U.S.—and Western—interests suggest Americans should be trying to go.

It is important to stress at the outset that the debate over U.S. policy in Central America is *not*, as the Administration so often claims, a debate over whether or not to assert U.S. power and influence in the region. It is a debate over *how best* to use U.S. power and influence to ensure that developments are more, rather than less, favorable to U.S. interests. It is a debate over how to use U.S. leverage, in what proportion, and for what purposes.

---

[2] "Communist Interference in El Salvador," U.S. Department of State, February 23, 1981, p. 8.

Origins and Implications of the Crisis: "North-South" or "East-West"?

There is a rather silly debate going on in Washington over whether Central America is a "North-South" issue or an "East-West" issue. This is how the policymaking community debates the issues when it chooses not to debate them on their own merits.

What is a North-South issue? The definition is elusive, but presumably those who employ this term mean that the Central American crisis arises from political, economic and social problems of that region that are common to the less developed countries—i.e., the South. If that is what is meant, then surely it is not debatable that Central America is a North-South problem. If Central America had been blessed for the past 50 years with responsive political systems, effective governments that respected human rights, equitable income distribution, and viable economies, it is difficult to imagine that we would be facing the problems that we now face there.

On the other hand, what is an East-West issue? Definitions are again elusive, but presumably it refers to the idea that the conflicts in Central America entail opportunities for geopolitical gains and risks of geopolitical losses by the Soviet Union and its allies on the one hand and by the United States and its allies, on the other. If that is what is meant, then surely it is no less clear that Central America is an East-West problem as well. Indeed, in a very real sense it is the East-West dimension of the Central American conflicts that *makes* them an issue for the United States. If the United States had no enemies in the world who could profit from Central America's travails, so much time would not be spent on the problem.

It can be left to the theorists of revolution to explain why revolutions arise and succeed or fail in particular times and places. But at a very basic level, it is possible to make one assertion with a great deal of confidence: most revolutions have essentially internal causes but attract external actors. In the current Central American circumstances, that gives the problem both East-West and North-South dimensions. That is a mere truism. To state it does not get us very far in determining what to *do* about the problem.

The consensus among knowledgeable people outside the Administration that the root causes of Central America's conflicts are local and regional in nature is so broad and deep that it is not really an issue. As one who has chaired dozens of congressional hearings on Central America over the past four years, I can attest that there are very few recognized experts in the United States who are prepared to defend the Reagan Administration's position that the instability is caused by Moscow and Havana. Most students of the region agree that armed leftist movements in Central America are basically a product of a destabilizing pattern of economic growth followed by economic decline and harsh repression of democratic reform movements. The pattern of economic growth that Central America experienced from 1950 to 1978 widened income disparities, pushing people off the land and driving them into unemployment and underemployment in urban slums. Politicians, labor and peasant leaders, intellectuals, and others who tried to represent the grievances of the dispossessed in the political process were routinely slaughtered.

No serious person could maintain that there is no international involvement in Central America's troubles. Central America has always been a theater of competition among the great powers. The Anglo-American rivalry of the nineteenth century has been supplanted in our own time by a Soviet-American rivalry. Obviously, the Soviets and the Cubans have supported guerrilla groups opposing U.S.-backed governments in the region. But, if I may be permitted to quote from one of my own speeches, Fidel Castro did not plant this garden; he is just shaking the trees and waiting for the ripe fruit to fall into his hands.

The Russians, the Cubans, and even the Sandinistas, did not cause the downfall of Anastasio Somoza Debayle. His fall was the result of an entire society rising up against a dictatorship that was no longer tolerable. The Sandinistas happened to be in a better position to seize power than were those who joined them in the overthrow, but if no one had joined them, they would in all probability still be in the hills. And as for the international aspect, Somoza's overthrow was aided, abetted, and heralded by a variety of countries friendly to the United States, including Venezuela, Panama, Costa Rica, even Honduras.

Domino Theories and Other Security Concerns

Proving that the United States has no monopoly on domino theories, the Cubans, the Sandinistas, and Marxist-Leninists throughout the region were convinced that Somoza's downfall presaged the long-awaited fall of the old order throughout Central America. They were right, but not in the way that they thought. The traditional Central American dictatorships do seem—one may hope—to be on their way out, consigned to the dustbin of history. But the march of socialism does not look quite so inevitable anymore. The 1981 final offensive of the Salvadoran guerrillas fizzled, and the conflict has settled into a stalemate. Stepped-up revolution in Guatemala only succeeded in bringing down on the Guatemalan people an outpouring of government terror that has left the country, for the time being, effectively "pacified." A guerrilla movement has failed to take hold in the less repressive and more open society of Honduras. Costa Rican democracy has thus far survived Sandinista meddling. Indeed, the principal effect of the Cubans' and Nicaraguans' overplaying their hand has been to bring down on the region not a revolution without borders, but an unprecedented U.S. military presence.

This analysis bears on the question of the security threats that the situation in Central America poses for the United States. Insofar as Central America has an East-West dimension, what is the extent of that dimension? The argument tends to be that security threats arise automatically from the takeover of Central American countries by Marxist-Leninist regimes allied with Cuba and the Soviet Union. However, while everyone agrees that that would be a highly undesirable outcome, it is difficult to pin down the precise security threats that it would create. The ones usually advanced turn out upon analysis to be more rationalizations than real threats.

This issue is relevant in this context because one of the security arguments made by the right rests, curiously, on the same domino theory employed by the left: that the success of one Marxist-Leninist revolution in Central America will inevitably produce the "fall" of the other Central American states, perhaps Panama, and in the more extreme versions, even Mexico. As noted, however, the history of the past five years in Central America gives us no reason to believe this. The evidence suggests that revolution is basically not "exportable." There is no case in history where groups of countries have fallen, like dominoes, to communism except through the direct intervention of the Soviet Army. Despite predictions to the contrary, it did not happen in Southeast Asia after the North Vietnamese victory, it did not happen in the Caribbean after the Castro revolution, and it has not happened in Central America.

The domino theory is inoperative for several reasons, but the main reason—curiously unrecognized by the theory's proponents—is the failure of the very revolutions whose spread the domino theory posits as inevitable. Five years ago it was widely thought that Central America faced a revolutionary future, that the left—hopefully, but not necessarily, the democratic left—would replace discredited rightist dictatorships. Now, however, it is the left that is discredited. Contrary to the expectations, Honduras and Costa Rica have moved to the right. The Farabundo Marti National Liberation Front has failed to win the international support it had hoped for.

While the Reagan Administration is obviously pleased with these trends, it cannot claim credit for them, because they are due principally to the left's own failures—specifically, to the failure of the Sandinista revolution, which hangs like an albatross on the Central American left. The hopes of the democratic left, that the Sandinistas would provide a model of humane revolution that threatened only through its example, have been dashed by the repression, the subversion, and the military buildup engaged in by the Sandinista government. Throughout Central America, Nicaragua is now feared not by military dictators, but by democratic leaders. The right is strengthened and the left hobbled by people's fear that it will bring a Sandinista future to their countries. It is not just the United States that refuses to tolerate the Sandinista regime; it is Nicaragua's neighbors as well who view continued Sandinista rule as incompatible with their security. If there are dominoes falling in Central America today, they would appear to be falling on Nicaragua.

Perhaps the most frequently reiterated security concern posed by the Administration that would follow from a Marxist-Leninist takeover of Central America is a purported threat to the Caribbean sea-lanes, through which much of U.S. commerce passes and which would be essential to resupply efforts in the event of a war in Europe or the Middle East. But, while most people are prepared to concede the strategic importance of the sea-lanes, it is far from clear how the political coloration of Central America would cause them to be significantly more or less at risk than they already are, given Soviet submarine capabilities and bases on Cuba. The capacity to threaten the sea-lanes arises not from the mere fact of the existence of Marxist-Leninist regimes in the region, but rather from the access that such regimes might give to Soviet military capabilities. Unless one makes the assumption that the latter is a necessary and unavoidable outcome of the former, it is difficult to see how the security of the Caribbean sea-lanes could become a significant issue with respect to Central America.

Another threat frequently mentioned by the Administration is the creation of massive migration to the United States. It is difficult to evaluate this thesis because of the absence of current and reliable data on migration from the region. The least that can be said, however, is that data to support the thesis that Marxist-Leninist regimes in Central America would cause significantly higher migration to the United States than would occur in the absence of such regimes do not appear to exist. All of the small, poor, economically dependent societies of the Caribbean Basin produce significant migration to the United States regardless of their forms of government. It could be argued that communist countries would *reduce* this flow by prohibiting emigration. I know of no reliable evidence that would suggest that the rate of migration from Cuba to the United States is higher than that for the other Caribbean islands, or that Nicaragua has produced more migrants than El Salvador. A communist takeover of Central America might increase migration to the United States but so might a lot of other factors—including a policy of repression designed to preclude a communist takeover. In short, the case is again difficult to make convincingly.

In fact, the only concrete security concern with respect to Central America on which there is a consensus in the United States is that the emplacement in the region of a Soviet strategic military capability that could threaten the United States would pose an unacceptable risk to U.S. security. However, that would not necessarily be the outcome if Marxist-Leninist regimes were to predominate in Central America and, in any case, it would not be a difficult threat to deal with. The United States certainly has the capability to remove such a threat, and would have considerable domestic and international support in doing so—although it would require a temporary diversion of U.S. forces from other missions. (It is worth noting in this regard that the Soviets have, by formal protocol, agreed to the Treaty of Tlatelolco, which bans the production, emplacement, or storage of nuclear weapons throughout Latin America.)

The United States does have important security concerns in Central America, but they have been obscured by the Reagan Administration's apocalyptic rhetoric. Every increment of Soviet military resources in the region undercuts the "economy of force" doctrine—the assumption of U.S. strategic theory that the Caribbean Basin will be a secure area. The inapplicability of the domino theory should not blind Americans to the real security costs that are imposed on the region, and on them, by the advent of hostile Marxist-Leninist regimes in Central America. Such regimes may give the Soviets footholds in the region that they could use to extend their influence further at U.S. expense. The basically pro-American coloration of Central America would be further threatened. The fact that revolutions are not necessarily exportable does not stop revolutionary regimes from trying, and the attempt obviously imposes costs on neighboring governments. The Sandinista revolution and the reaction to it by the United States and by Nicaragua's neighbors have created an arms race in the region that imposes further costs. A Soviet-armed Nicaragua with possible regional ambitions cannot be taken lightly. If a revolutionary regime were to take power in Guatemala, Mexico would not automatically topple like a domino, but Mexico could well encounter increased problems with its Indian population in the south; this would not pose a mortal threat, but it would impose a substantial cost. Even though it is unlikely that any combination of Central American states could seriously threaten the Panama Canal, a more radicalized and militarized Central America would presumably require new assumptions about the cost of defending the Canal.

Furthermore, most Americans, myself included (and, I daresay, most Europeans), would view Marxist-Leninist takeovers of Central American countries as highly undesirable for less concrete reasons. For one thing, most Americans want what is best for other people in the world, and most Americans do not think that includes living under communist regimes. The Administration's rhetoric about its critics notwithstanding, Americans are really agreed on that. For another, Americans understand intuitively that the *perception* of U.S. security—the perception of the United States as a country in control of its destiny—would inevitably be affected, regardless of the concrete effects on sea-lanes, refugee flows, or the security of the other countries of the region.

The problem remains, however: the assertion that Central America has a security dimension for the United States does not get Washington anywhere in determining what to do about Central America as a matter of policy. In particular, in the American political debate, the assertion of security concerns with respect to Central America tends to be misused to support military solutions. But it does not necessarily follow that security concerns are best addressed solely or even primarily with military means. In the Central American case, I would argue the contrary: to the extent that the aforementioned security concerns are real, the way to deal with those concerns is through constructive, responsible diplomatic initiatives. In order more effectively to advance perceived U.S. security interests, the United States must develop a greater appreciation of the local roots of Central America's conflicts. In other words, in order to be more effective on the East-West dimension of the problem, the United States must develop a greater appreciation of the North-South dimension. The two dimensions are linked: the United States enhances its security by dealing with the region in a more realistic manner.

U.S., European, and Soviet Interests in Central America

Given the situation in Central America, what are the interests of the several actors with respect to this region? It is often asserted that the United States has "vital interests" in Central America. But the concept of vital interests is a very slippery one, the more so as the term is debased in political debate. Trying to reserve some special meaning for the concept, one might ask: What interests does the United States have in the region that it could legitimately go to war to defend? That would entail, presumably, a direct threat to the country. And do Western Europe or the Soviet Union have vital interests in the region in this sense?

I have already argued that it is difficult to identify vital interests that the United States has in Central America. The United States is not dependent on Central America in any sense, and no combination of Central American countries could threaten the security of the United States. The only vital interest of the United States in Central America that most Americans would appear to agree on is the interest in preventing the emplacement of outside military capabilities in the region that could directly threaten the United States. Other powers outside the Hemisphere must speak for themselves, but I am unable to identify any vital interest of the European countries or the Soviet Union in Central America.

The concept of vital interests is not helpful with respect to Central America. The countries of the region are too small, too poor, and too weak for the major powers to have any truly vital interests there. Use of the concept tends to denigrate real U.S. interests in the region, which in my view are fundamentally political. The United States seeks in Central America a region of states that see major issues more or less as it does. To the extent that it can achieve that, Washington virtually automatically protects any other interests that Americans might have. These political interests cannot be called "vital" in the traditional sense of the word, but they *are* the *primary* interests of the United States in the region. It would be counterproductive to attempt to achieve these interests by means of war, but Washington ought to pursue them vigorously by all appropriate means.

Accordingly, the United States should be prepared to make a rather significant commitment of resources to fostering democracy, economic growth, equitable and participatory development, respect for human rights, and regional stability in Central America. These are important political interests. To the extent that there is success in achieving them, significant benefits will accrue both to the United States and to the people of Central America. Conversely, marginal gains will be denied to the Soviets. In fact, the best long-term way to protect U.S. strategic interests in Central America is to do a good job of promoting these political interests there. Soviet ability to threaten U.S. strategic interests would be very limited in a region of healthy, prosperous, equitable democracies.

The other powers would again have to speak for themselves, but European interests on this level might include the absence of a situation in Central America that would divert U.S. attention from Europe and its defense, and the maintenance of European political and economic ties to the region. And to judge from its behavior, the Soviet Union perceives an interest in distracting and embarrassing the United States and gaining footholds in Central America through the opportunistic manipulation of instability, discontent, and anti-American sentiment generated by U.S. backing of reactionary regimes in the region.

The actors also possess other, less tangible interests in the region, which are affected by the effectiveness with which they pursue their more concrete interests. The United States, and the West generally, persumably share an interest in demonstrating the efficacy of Western approaches to government and development—an interest that exists with respect to other Third World regions as well. Soviet ideology would suggest a Soviet interest in seeing events in Central America that would support the doctrine of the inevitable march to socialism; however, there is no evidence that the Soviets are prepared to pay any significant price to grease the skids of history in this regard.

One of these less tangible factors is credibility, the preservation of which is often mentioned as an interest of the United States that is at stake in Central America. This too is a very slippery concept. Many Americans would agree that U.S. credibility is in some sense involved in Central America; but they would differ strongly on *how* that credibility is engaged, and on the implications for policy. Credibility is a very subjective concept; like beauty, it exists primarily in the eye of the beholder. Whether a situation affects U.S. credibility depends in large part on whether the United States says it does. Consternation over the supposed U.S. loss of credibility because of the fall of Somoza is heard mainly in the United States. It is more a matter of domestic than international concern. In Latin America, the fall of Somoza was viewed as a minus for the United States only by a few other military dictatorships that feared their turn was next. Since Somoza's fall was in fact widely favored and heralded throughout most of the Hemisphere, what has raised doubts about the United States was not the fall itself but how the United States handled the fall and its aftermath. The intelligent pursuit of its interests obviously enhances U.S. credibility in the world, but that generalization leaves unanswered the difficult question of what the intelligent pursuit of U.S. interests actually entails. The question of interests brings up the concept of spheres of influence. Should the fact that Central America is in the United States' "backyard" and not in other countries' "backyards" affect the respective interests of nations? Should the United States insist on deference from the other powers for this reason? Is U.S. credibility more at risk in this region than elsewhere *because* Central America is viewed as within the United States' "backyard"? Should Central America be viewed as a U.S. sphere of influence, or not?

The answers are complex. The geographical location of Central America clearly has implications for the kinds and degrees of interest that outside powers will have in the region. It obviously matters to the United States—at least, it should—whether Marxist-led revolution occurs near its borders or in a distant part of the world. Equally obvious, the United States is prepared to tolerate Soviet capabilities on the Soviet periphery that it is not prepared to tolerate near its own periphery.

But the concept of spheres of influence must be used with care. The idea that the United States has special security interests in Central America, in part because of its geographical relationship to the area, is well accepted by most Central Americans as well as by friends and adversaries of the United States outside the area. The idea that that gives Washington *carte blanche* to dictate the political and economic configuration of the area is not accepted. To try to seal the region off from non-Hemispheric influence and impose ideological conformity would require a pervasive form of control that no American could look forward to with any pride. The attempt would damage U.S. credibility, not enhance it.

The Reagan Administration's Policy: Hegemony and Its Implications

Most Americans would prefer a region of friendly, equitable democracies, at peace with each other and with the United States, economically healthy, and respectful of human rights. These are universal objectives to which most Americans give at least lip service. And these are the objectives that Americans tend to have in mind when they say that they do not disagree on objectives, only on the means for accomplishing them.

Unfortunately, those objectives have thus far proven unachievable in much of the world, and even less so in Central America than in many other places. Because diplomacy, like politics, is the art of the possible, its practitioners must necessarily focus on more finite, "operational objectives," or guiding principles, to steer decision-making. And there seems to be a rather fundamental disagreement between the Administration and its critics at the level of operational objectives.

The Administration's operational objective in Central America has been aptly put by former Assistant Secretary for Inter-American Affairs Viron Vaky: to reestablish U.S. hegemony over the region. What this means is that the United States will reassert its presumed prerogative of determining the limits within which the Central American republics may operate politically, economically, and internationally. Operationally, for the Administration this means that leftist regimes, and even regimes with significant leftist participation, are ruled out. Other criteria for the acceptance or rejection of Central American political patterns follow naturally from that single guiding principle: no ties with Cuba; private-sector-oriented development strategies; support for the regional and international positions of the United States; etc. Other objectives play a secondary role: democracy, equitable development, and respect for human rights. These exist less as independent values than as instruments of—and verbal rationalizations for—the pursuit of hegemony. This operational objective is not necessarily shared by everyone in the Administration, and not all Administration behavior is consistent with it. But the objective clearly reflects the "ideological center of gravity" within the Administration.

This guiding principle of reestablishing American hegemony has a series of effects for U.S. policy in the region. First, it provides an answer to the question of whether the Sandinista regime can be tolerated. The answer is no. The Administration has made clear that it will only deal with the Sandinista regime if it becomes another kind of regime. Until then, operational policy is to try to intimidate the Sandinistas into making or permitting such a change in regime. To the Administration, containment is not enough. U.S. policy is to attempt to alter the fundamental character of the regime—through intimidation if possible, but perhaps by removing the regime if necessary.

The United States has over the past four years engaged in a series of actions designed to implement its conclusion that the Sandinista regime cannot be tolerated. It has sought to isolate Nicaragua, not only diplomatically, but also economically, in an attempt to induce a change in its political regime by increasing economic deprivation and discontent. It has sought to exacerbate political contradictions within Nicaragua, in an attempt to induce a change in regime by increasing political discontent. It has sought to induce a change in regime through military threats and intimidation: the United States has created an armed exile force to fight within the country; and it has held large, highly visible, overtly threatening military maneuvers, a by-product of which has been the creation of the necessary infrastructure in the region for eventual direct U.S. military intervention in Nicaragua.

Second, the guiding principle provides an answer to the question of the role of Western Europe and the regional Latin American powers. That role is minimal at best. Ideally, the Administration would like to have active support for its policy. But since most of the other powers in question do not see Central America as the Reagan Administration does or share U.S. objectives for the region, this is impossible. Therefore, the Administration has had to settle for a policy of trying to keep outside powers from complicating or actively opposing U.S. policy.

It has not always been successful. The French-Mexican declaration of 1982 was a significant attack on U.S. policy. Members of the Contadora Group, (which was born in opposition to U.S. policy and whose raison d'être is fundamentally at variance with U.S. operational objectives) have spoken out against the large U.S. exercises and naval maneuvers in 1983, the mining of Nicaragua's harbors in 1984, and the Administration's failure later in 1984 to support a draft treaty that Nicaragua had agreed to sign. Several European leaders—particularly Prime Minister Felipe González of Spain—worked very hard to achieve an agreement between the Sandinista government and the Coordinadora Democratica Nacional for free elections in Nicaragua, at a time when, according to a *New York Times* report, the Central Intelligence Agency was working against that agreement.[3]

The Administration's attitude toward these activities is suggested by the remark of a senior Administration official, in response to European criticism of the mining of Nicaragua's harbors, that Europeans are not properly appreciative of U.S. security concerns. But that is not the case. The United States' European and Contadora friends do these things because they take a longer term view. They know that the restoration of U.S. hegemony is not a viable strategy in the long run; therefore, they seek arrangements that will protect U.S. interests in other ways.

But disturbed as they are by U.S. policy, both the European and the regional powers have generally been reluctant to confront the United States directly with respect to Central America. The Europeans have more important concerns, and they recognize that Central America is an area of primary concern to the United States. The regional powers recognize that they cannot achieve their objectives in the region without the cooperation of the United States; they also have overwhelming problems of their own on which they seek U.S. assistance, and they fear U.S. reprisals if they exercise too much independence. The United States has been able fairly easily to defuse any potential threat arising from the involvement of regional powers by symbolically supporting their objectives in its rhetoric while adhering steadfastly to policies that make the achievement of those objectives impossible.

Third, the guiding principle provides an answer to the question of the proper mix of various foreign policy instruments in the conduct of U.S. foreign policy toward the region. In this respect as in the others, however, it is important to go beyond official U.S. government justifications and get to the reality underneath. The Administration makes a lot of the fact that its economic assistance requests exceed its military assistance requests, thereby creating the impression that its priority is on the economic dimension and not the military one. But more important than the number of dollars assigned to each category of aid are the policy objectives that

---

[3] Philip Taubman, "U.S. Role in Nicaragua Vote Disputed," *The New York Times*, October 21, 1984, p. 12.

the aid is designed to serve. Seen in this light, it is clear that U.S. economic aid to the region is designed principally to serve U.S. military objectives.

U.S. economic aid to El Salvador has the primary purpose of keeping the Salvadoran economy afloat so that the government can continue to fight the war. This hardly constitutes giving priority to El Salvador's underlying economic problems, none of which are being—or can be—attacked under the current circumstances. U.S. economic aid to Honduras serves essentially as a payoff to the Honduran government for permitting the United States to use Honduras for U.S. geopolitical objectives in the region—a bargain that the Honduran government occasionally makes embarrassingly clear by its statements that the United States is not giving it enough economic aid to uphold its end of the deal. The United States has sought to strike a similiar bargain with Costa Rica, but Costa Rica has, with some success, resisted being drawn into U.S. strategic plans in the region.

Fourth, the guiding principle provides an answer to the question of what the role should be for negotiations leading to political and diplomatic settlements, as proposed by the Contadora Group and others. It is crucial to be clear on what this answer is. With respect to Nicaragua, no diplomatic settlement is possible unless there is a change in regime in Managua because, without such a change, a diplomatic settlement would entail acceptance of the regime. With respect to El Salvador, no political settlement is possible because it would necessarily entail the involvement and participation of the left. Lip service is given to the idea of negotiated settlements as a symbolic value, but in four years U.S. policy has not budged an inch in the operational content that it gives to this idea: a negotiated settlement with the Sandinista regime is possible only if it ceases to be the Sandinista regime; and the only thing to be negotiated in El Salvador is the terms of the left's surrender. In short, U.S. policy leaves no room for settlements at all.

At an abstract level there is nothing particularly wrong with the Administration's operational objective in Central America. From the Administration's point of view, there are a variety of arguments in its favor. First, in the Administration's world view, either the Russians will control Central America or the United States will, and given that choice, it had better be the United States.

Second, elites can certainly be found in Central America that would readily accept U.S. hegemony. Third, put simply: why not? For good and proper reasons of national security, the United States has sought to dominate the Caribbean Basin; if it can continue to dominate, why not do so?

However, when one steps down from the abstract level and analyzes the actual effects of this objective—the actual effects of the attempt to reimpose hegemony—one sees that the policy has counterproductive effects militating against U.S. interests in the region. In short, the policy simply does not work.On the Administration's own evidence Nicaragua is less pluralistic, more dependent on Cuba, and more feared by its neighbors today than it was when the Administration took office. Those in the Sandinista movement who were taught by ideology and history that the United States would inevitably sponsor a counter-revolution have been proved right. Hence, their invocation of that threat, in classic Marxist-Leninist fashion, to justify seizing control of the society and cracking down on dissent, has also been vindicated. It is undoubtedly true, as many argue, that there were strong forces pushing the Sandinista revolution in that direction apart from U.S. pressure. Certainly, it is the Sandinistas, not the United States, who are fundamentally responsible for Nicaragua's problems. But that does not excuse a U.S. policy that encourages events to evolve in a direction in which one says one does not want them to go.

In El Salvador it seems elementary from any analysis of history that the way to prove wrong the Cuban-Sandinista faith in the inevitable spread of the revolution—their version of the domino theory—is to work to stop the repression and to foster the development of a political system in which people who were driven out by repression can return and participate. The best way to prove them right is to support continued repression and killing, and to avoid opening up avenues of political participation for the left. It is therefore curious in the extreme that, at least during its first three years, the Administration chose the latter policy. It aided and abetted the steady rightward drift of a Salvadoran political system that remained firmly in the hands of the military. Throughout that period, the death squads operated with impunity, and year in and year out the Salvadoran armed forces killed more unarmed civilian noncombatants than they did guerrillas. Hundreds were imprisoned without trial for political offenses; many were tortured. And through it all, every overture of the left to talk about the terms under which it would return to participate in the political process was firmly rebuffed.

With respect to Honduras, U.S. policy has succeeded neither in strengthening the security of the country nor in fostering democracy and development. On the contrary, by deliberately implicating Honduras in the region's conflicts by using it as a base for the "contras" and other forms of anti-Nicaraguan activity, U.S. policy has increased Honduras' *insecurity*. And by financing a huge military buildup in that country, U.S. policy has increased the power of the military vis-à-vis civilian actors in the political process, greatly increased the opportunities for and the stakes of corruption in what was already one of Central America's most corrupt militaries, and abetted a diversion of resources away from economic development and the alleviation of poverty. The chosen instrument of the United States in Honduras, former Commander in Chief of the Armed Forces General Gustavo Alvarez Martínez, has been implicated in the repression of political dissent in Honduras and in an upsurge in the practices of kidnapping and secret detention.

These are the counterproductive consequences of a hegemonic policy. Having determined that the United States cannot live with the Sandinistas, but unwilling (as of this writing) to face the costs of invading the country and removing them from power, the Reagan Administration is forced to continue applying pressures that are designed to intimidate the Sandinistas into changing their ways but that actually have the opposite effect. Having dismissed with the slogan "power sharing" any effective form of political participation by the Salvadoran left, and with no prospect of prevailing militarily at any level of commitment that it has thus far been prepared to make, the Administration is forced to continue a policy of escalation that only heightens those contradictions in Salvadoran society on which the guerrillas must ultimately depend for their success. Honduras and—one fears—even Costa Rica are in danger of being dragged down with the policy, and regional war remains a real possibility.

This military overreaction does not blunt Soviet long-term strategic objectives in the region; it aids them, by fostering anti-

Americanism and by failing to deal with the root causes of the instability and the economic nonviability on which Soviet strategy depends. If we do not want to continue down this road—and we should not—then we need a new operational objective that more adequately takes account of the realities of the region—a principle from which would flow more positive effects for ourselves, our allies, and the region.

In 1984 there were some hopeful developments on all these fronts—some fortuitous, some indicating that pragmatists within the Foreign Service may be succeeding in nudging Administration policy off its ideological moorings. In El Salvador these include the crackdown on the death squads and the election of José Napoleón Duarte to the presidency, and the peace talks launched by Duarte in La Palma in October. Less dramatic but at least as significant has been the rise to power within the armed forces of moderate reformists, led by Chief of Staff Col. Adolfo Blandón, who believe that ending human rights abuses and supporting dialogue with the left is in the interest of the survival of the armed forces as an institution. The visit of U.S. Secretary of State George Shultz to Managua in June and the resulting series of talks between U.S. Special Envoy Harry W. Schlaudeman and Nicaraguan Deputy Minister of Foreign Affairs Victor Hugo Tinoco, which continue at this writing, constitute a hopeful sign in U.S.-Nicaraguan relations. In Honduras, there are signs that the ouster of Alvarez may have improved the situation somewhat.

Whether these trends turn out to be temporary or long-lasting depends to a large extent on the policies of the second Reagan Administration. The U.S.-Nicaraguan talks and such support as the United States has given to President Duarte, human rights, and peace talks in El Salvador were widely viewed in the United States and Central America as ephemeral election-year phenomena. Unfortunately, the Administration did much to fuel and justify this perception.

U.S. support for Duarte's peace overture has been lukewarm at best, and many observers think it would have been even less positive had not Duarte brilliantly timed his move for three weeks before the U.S. election. There is no reason, so far, to believe that the United States has altered its objectives in El Salvador in a way that would make a negotiated settlement possible. U.S. efforts to curb the most visible human rights abuses—the death squad murders—came only after more than 40,000 deaths had occurred, and only when the Administration needed to shore up support at home for the vastly increased military aid recommended by the National Bipartisan Commission on Central America (i.e., the Kissinger Commission). Meanwhile, the Administration has continued to deny the existence of the most prevalent—but less visible—form of human rights abuse in El Salvador, the killing of civilian noncombatants in air force bombings and army sweeps, and to impugn the integrity of Salvadoran human rights organizations that report these abuses.

Hopes for the U.S.-Nicaraguan talks were undercut when the Administration was forced to lobby publicly against a Central American peace treaty drafted by the Contadora Group after Nicaragua had agreed to sign it. *The New York Times* reported that "Officials of the Administration said there was no way it would accept an agreement with the Sandinista Government as it is currently made up."[4] On separate occasions the *Times* further reported that the Central Intelligence Agency had worked to thwart an electoral agreement between Nicaragua's main opposition coalition and the Sandinista government, and that the U.S. Embassy in Managua had tried to get registered opposition parties to withdraw from the election.[5] Finally, with respect to Honduras, leaks have indicated that a resumption of large-scale military manuevers, possibly extending into El Salvador, is planned for the second term.

In short, the signs are at best ambiguous. At worst, they suggest that U.S. policy under the second Reagan Administration will remain fundamentally opposed to a political settlement in El Salvador and a Contadora agreement in Central America. If that proves to be the case, the only hope for peace will be for the countries of the region to increase their efforts to take their destiny into their own hands. That is, in essence, what the Contadora effort repre-

---

[4] Leslie H. Gelb, "Stalemates Will Survive the Election, *The New York Times*, October 8, 1984, p. A14.

[5] Taubman, *op. cit.*; and Stephen Kinzer, "Nicaraguan Parties Cite Sandinista Aid and U.S. Pressure," *The New York Times*, October 31, 1984, pp. 1 and 10.

sents, as does Duarte's peace initiative. The basic dynamic of U.S.-Central America relations during 1985 and beyond could well be defined by the effort of the United States to retain control, continuing to try to use its Central American allies for its purposes, versus the increasing efforts of the Central American and Contadora countries to pursue their own quite different agendas.

An Alternative Policy of Regional Settlement

The alternative operational objective that has been suggested by critics of the Administration centers on the idea of a regional settlement. The settlement principle derives from the simple proposition that if the exorcism of leftist influence from the region is unachievable at any cost that you are willing to pay, then you have to try to achieve a settlement with the left that the parties concerned can live with. More generally, if current policies are only making things worse, it makes sense to try alternative policies that might make things better.

The implications of this principle are not that the United States would cease to try to defend its security or to exercise influence in the region, but that it would do so in different ways, for more limited and more achievable objectives. The objectives can be limited precisely because the threats emanating from the region are, as argued in a preceding section, less grave than the Administration suggests.

Instead of trying to enforce political conformity by military means, the purpose, under this principle, would be to foster political and diplomatic settlements of Central America's conflicts of a sort that would enhance the position of political forces and parties compatible with U.S. interests and maximize the probablity that compatible values will prevail. Democracy, equitable development, and respect for human rights would move up in the U.S. hierarchy of objectives out of a recognition that they would contribute to the stability that it is in the American interest to see prevail in the region. Washington would still seek to minimize Central American ties with Cuba, promote the private sector, and gain support for the regional and international positions of the United States, but the use of military instruments to accomplish these objectives would be de-emphasized.

What effects would adoption of this guiding principle have on U.S. policy in the region? First, the principle would permit a much more sophisticated approach to the Sandinista regime. Under this approach, the United States would not necessarily rule out the use of force against the Sandinistas, depending on their behavior, but it would not rule out living with them either. Washington would say to the Sandinistas that it was prepared to negotiate and enter into mutually acceptable security arrangements with them and was ready to encourage U.S. allies to do the same. Policies that have been demonstrably and predictably ineffective in fostering political reconciliation, a more open political system, and respect for human rights in Nicaragua—indeed, policies that were not intended to do so—could be replaced by more nuanced ones specifically designed to encourage these trends.

Only time could tell whether the Sandinistas would accept such negotiations and whether this policy would be successful in moderating the regime. The United States has pursued counterproductive policies for four years, and it may be too late. It may not—probably will not—like the regime that it ends up having to live with under this policy. But that is the case with many Latin American and Third World regimes. At least the regime would no longer be able to blame its shortcomings on the United States. In any event, there is no alternative to this policy if Americans want to avoid war and begin to try to build stability in the region.

It should also be mentioned that, by working to decrease the tensions and contradictions in the region, such a policy would help take the steam out of other violent revolutions and reduce the likelihood that other leftist revolutionary movements would come to power.

In pursuing a policy of regional settlement, the roles of the other powers would be very different from what they are under current policies. Because the United States would be seeking settlements, rather than resisting them, the role of other powers that also seek such settlements would be enhanced. The Reagan Administration could encourage the Contadora Group to try to devise a series of settlements. It could encourage those countries in Central America most responsive to the United States to help achieve such settlements, rather than use them to thwart settlements, as has been the case. The Administration could seek to be helpful, and could pledge to support any settlement arrived at by the countries most immediately concerned that adequately protects U.S. interests. This may not work. But why rule out the possibility that the United States could be more successful in achieving its own interests in Central America by letting its friends try for a settlement than it has been in pursuing unilateral diplomacy?

In a similiar manner, this policy would lead to a change in the U.S. attitude toward West European involvement. Instead of resisting such involvement, for the Europeans do not support U.S. hegemonic intentions, the United States could encourage its allies to join it and the regional actors in the search for settlements. This way Washington would not be locked into an isolated position, pursuing its objectives in Central America through unilateral means.

A strategy of seeking regional settlements would open up the whole panoply of foreign policy instruments, including the use of military aid to achieve coherent foreign policy objectives. Washington would continue to confront Nicaragua with disincentives for behavior that it views as inimical to U.S. interests. But the United States would abandon mindless pressure on behalf of demands that can never be satisfied. It would continue to help the Salvadoran government to prevent its forceful overthrow by the guerrillas, but it would do this in the context of a strategy for ending the conflict. It would continue to help Honduras meet its legitimate security needs.

However, a policy of promoting a regional settlement would entail several changes in U.S. military aid strategy. First, the amounts would be less, since the purpose of the aid would be more limited. Second, the aid would be placed conspicuously at the service of achieving settlements. Aid to El Salvador, for example, would be conditioned on the government's willingness to work for a settlement with the left, instead of being used, as it is now, to reinforce military oppostion to a settlement. Third, aid would not be given, overtly or covertly, for the purpose of threatening the existence of other governments.Economic assistance would achieve a new prominence under a settlement strategy. Instead of having essentially the purpose of rewarding behavior that is inimical to settlements, as is the case now, economic aid would be used to promote settlements. Significant increases could be promised to countries that settle with their internal opposition and/or with their neighbors, thereby creating conditions of stability that would permit the aid to be used with real effect. Immediate balance-of-payments support could also be used to encourage rather than discourage settlements. More aid could be targeted directly on the alleviation of suffering.

The foreign policy instrument that would most dramatically be given new life by a settlement strategy is diplomacy. The United States is currently experiencing a kind of diplomatic immobilism. The purpose of U.S. diplomacy is not to reach agreements but to prevent them. Diplomacy is shackled, unable to exercise its traditional function of finding a "way out" because none is being sought. Under a settlement strategy, diplomacy would be liberated to seek ways short of war for furthering U.S. interests.

Finally, by definition, a settlement strategy would give primary emphasis to negotiations leading to political and diplomatic settlements. Its very purpose would be to achieve an accommodation with Nicaragua and a political settlement with the Salvadoran left, if such be possible. The reason for this would not be to give in to the Sandinistas and the Salvadoran left, but precisely to contain them by drawing them into political and diplomatic processes with conditions of participation that would preclude the forms of behavior the United States finds most worrisome. A recent historical example drawn from the region well illustrates the efficacy of this strategy. There was a time when Washington responded in a sophisticated and constructive manner to demands for change in the region, and it has paid off handsomely. I refer to the United States' willingness to negotiate the Panama Canal Treaties. That single act has done more to enhance U.S. security in Central America than everything the United States has done there since. And this was accomplished not by shortsightedly insisting that "the Canal has always been ours, and it will remain ours," but by accommodating Panamanian demands in a way that protects the U.S. interest in the Canal. At the same time this approach defused an anti-U.S. reaction in Panama and the rest of the region and enabled those countries to remain politically friendly to Washington. The United States was able to safeguard its security interests by protecting its political interests through responsible diplomacy. Unfortunately, those who now control U.S. foreign policy opposed those treaties, and they continue to oppose flexible responses to change that could similiarly protect U.S. interests.

In contrast, another recent historical example drawn from the region illustrates how the United States magnifies its security problems by failing to act with sufficient vigor on the diplomatic front. The United States is now reduced to trying to remove the Sandinistas from power in Nicaragua by military means. But if it had used more vigorous diplomacy prior to July 1979, the Sandinistas might never have achieved power and the moderates might have been in power today. The Sandinistas were able to take power because the situation had been allowed to deteriorate to the point where the moderates were no longer a viable force, and the idea that evolutionary change was possible was discredited. As this deterioration occurred, the United States was unable to get its diplomatic act together. Fearing that the alternatives to Somoza would be worse, the United States vacillated on withdrawing its support from him—thereby maximizing the possibilities that the alternative would be worse. The United States might have been able to use its influence in an enlightened, effective way to avoid polarization and arrest the development of a revolutionary situation, but it failed to do so. Once again, those who argued most strongly that the U.S. government had to stick with Somoza to the end to avoid a worse alternative are now in power, and continue to resist the use of diplomacy to deal with revolutionary situations.

Now the United States faces another situation in which its active support for constructive diplomatic efforts could be helpful. The Contadora Group has proposed a series of agreements covering nonaggression, troop levels, foreign advisers, verification, and democratization that could, if accepted and implemented, satisfy the security concerns of the countries of the region. The Contadora efforts have not borne fruit because of the failure of key actors—regrettably including the United States—to back the group's efforts. The United States insists on pursuing goals of its own, principally the demise of the Sandinista regime, which cannot be achieved through multilateral diplomacy. This shortsighted unilateralism is a substitute for—not, as is so often thought, synonymous with—the vigorous pursuit of U.S. interests. A less direct role by the United States would not constitute abdication of its responsibilities or a less active search for arrangements that would serve its interests. On the contrary, vigorous U.S. support of regional mechanisms for Latin American participation in the resolution of Central American conflicts would open up new possibilities for achieving U.S. interests.

The Question of Military Intervention

It is fair to ask, however: What happens if diplomacy fails? What happens if a genuine settlement strategy does not produce settlements—as it well may not? Should the United States forswear, unconditionally and forever, the option of using military force in this region? If not, under what conditions should force be employed, and what effects would that have in Central America, in Latin America generally, and in Europe?

It is very difficult—and, from a diplomatic point of view, of doubtful utility—to attempt to set forth in advance the precise circumstances under which the United States should intervene directly with military force in Central America. Circumstances rarely occur precisely as anticipated; moreover, is almost impossible to state the circumstances with sufficient precision to avoid problems later on. If the conditions under which Washington would intervene are defined too tightly, they will encourage challenges that fall just short of the behavior that the United States announces will trigger the use of force. If the conditions are defined too loosely, the United States risks having its bluff called. Nevertheless, it is worth thinking about what these conditions are, if for no other reason than that, under current circumstances, the American people and their allies need reassurance about Washington's intention to use force at least as much as its adversaries do.

There are very few circumstances that would justify the *unilateral* use of military force by the United States in Central America. This is so for essentially three reasons: first, the historical legacy of U.S. relations with the Caribbean Basin is such that it is almost impossible for the use of force in that region by the United States to be well received; second, the nature of the problems that the United States has to address in the region is such as to make the unilateral use of force generally inappropriate; and third, better alternatives exist.

The only circumstances that would necessitate and justify unilateral military intervention by the United States in Central America would be (1) the emplacement of offensive Soviet military capabilities in the region that could directly threaten the United States; (2) an immediate threat to the lives or safety of U.S. citizens; and (3) an invasion of Central America by a power outside the region. Even in the third case, unilateral U.S. intervention would probably not be necessary, because regional mechanisms exist whereby the United States could respond under multilateral auspices to precisely such a challenge.

Lower level threats—i.e., threats to one country by another within the region—can best be dealt with at the regional level. The Contadora countries and—particularly because of U.S. aid programs—the Central American countries are perfectly capable of dealing with Nicaragua themselves. If direct U.S. assistance is necessary—as it might be, for example, in the case of Costa Rica, which has no means of self-defense—such assistance should be provided under the collective security mechanisms of the Organization of American States that exist for that purpose. There are no foreseeable circumstances under which it would be necessary or justified for the United States to occupy a Central American country or remove its government by force. The response should be proportional to the threat. The United States only delegitimizes an otherwise legitimate objective by seeming to use it as an excuse to occupy a country. If force is used only as a last resort, with a clear sense of proportion, for legitimate and unambiguous purposes and, whenever possible, under regional mechanisms in circumstances where more directly affected allies are genuinely taking the lead, then the effect on U.S. relations with Latin America and Europe would be minimal. If those limits are not adhered to, then the potential would exist for severely damaging U.S. relations with Europe and—particularly—Latin America, and for getting into the position of an occupying power, a position from which extrication is not easy. The possibility that the United States would have to intervene directly under the criteria laid out above is extremely remote, assuming that the United States genuinely seeks through responsible diplomacy to avoid having to resort to force.

Central America and the Atlantic Alliance

What effect does all this have on alliance relations? My own guess is: not very much. The alliance has a very high tolerance for the behavior—even the misguided behavior—of its members in the areas of special concern to a given member but marginal to the alliance.

It is fortunate, if it is true, that the way in which the United States deals with Central America will have only a marginal effect on the alliance, because it is unlikely that *any* U.S. policy in Central America is going to inspire a great deal of confidence among the other members of the Western Alliance. The problems are intractable, and there are no good options left. Generations of U.S. support for the old order in Central America are finally coming home to roost as that order crumbles and the United States scrambles, too late, to regain some control of events, reimpose order, and channel the political evolution of the region within acceptable bounds. The divestiture of empire was a messy and unseemly affair for all the alliance members who had to go through it, and there is no reason to expect the United States to accept its loss of hegemony over Central America with any more aplomb. Furthermore, as there is no unity of opinion on the matter in Europe, to some extent the United States will be damned no matter which way it turns.

Nevertheless, West Europeans do have views on these matters, and there are ways in which the United States can handle its Central America problem so as to minimize losses in alliance confidence and strains in alliance relations. Europeans must speak for themselves with respect to what they hope for and expect from the United States in its handling of its Central America problem. But from my contact with Europeans, it seems that what they most want is some sense that the United States knows what it is doing. They do not want the Cubanization of Central America, nor do they want another Vietnam there. Most of all, they want the United States to pursue its interests in the region intelligently—to act in Central America with some realism, with some decent regard for the facts, with some sense of proportion and some maturity, as befits a great power. They are dismayed by the political polarization in the United States that prevents the carrying out of a coherent U.S. policy with respect to Central America, and they fear drastic shifts in that policy with each change in administration. They want to support the United States, but they do not know what U.S. policy is—and as soon as they figure it out, it changes.

In this light, it seems to me that Europeans must be alarmed at a U.S. policy that appears out of control in Central America. They see rampant military escalation on all fronts, coupled with the closing off of possibilities for realistic political and diplomatic solutions, while at the same time the U.S. position in the region deteriorates. They see a United States seemingly pursuing open-ended objectives that cannot be accomplished with the means being employed, which makes them wonder what Washington will do next. Europeans must have doubts about the wisdom of U.S. judgments, and about the soundness of a political system that can produce such judgments. They know the Soviet threat is real; hence their concern not that the United States imagines the threat but that it might shoot itself in the foot in attempting to deal with the threat. If Washington sought the Europeans' help in bringing about solutions, instead of claiming a right to European acquiescence to U.S. policies about which the Europeans have deep doubts, it would help the alliance.

The Domestic Context of U.S. Policy

Why does the United States behave as it does in Central America? In particular, why does it pursue counterproductive policies? Why does it get so "locked in"? Why do U.S. policies seem to so many of its friends in Europe to be out of proportion and out of control? Why are its policies the subject of so much domestic political infighting? Why do its friends worry about violent swings in U.S. policies? What is the possibility of achieving changes in policy that would make the United States more credible to friend and foe alike?

As a practicing politician, I tend to operate on the theory that domestic politics drives foreign policy just as it does other types of policy. This becomes particularly clear with respect to areas, such as Central America, that Americans do not understand well, and with respect to which they share no clear conception of U.S. interests. That tends to heighten the influence of domestic political factors in U.S. policy.

There has long been a fundamental duality in the U.S. approach to change in the Third World, which in turn reflects a duality in the way Americans think about themselves. On the one hand, the United States was born in a revolution that was fought in the name of revolutionary political ideals that it judged to have universal applicability. Americans believe that mankind still aspires to achieve the ideals that they fought for more than 200 years ago, and that belief has created a strain of sympathy in them for revolutions against foreign masters or domestic dictators.

On the other hand, there has arisen a distinctly status-quo-oriented, anti-revolutionary tradition in U.S. policy toward the Third World, particularly as the United States developed economic interests that were threatened by revolutionary change. In the post-World War II era of U.S.-Soviet global competition, this side of the American "character" has come to be epitomized by anti-communism—for more than 30 years the centerpiece of American foreign policy. Americans have been convinced that they were locked with the Soviet Union in a death struggle for control of the world. At the same time, revolutions have taken on a Marxist character. Accordingly, Americans have been caught between their natural sympathy for the desire of peoples for change to meet indigenous aspirations, and their feeling that they had to oppose revolutions that would benefit "communists."

The tension between the revolutionary, pro-change side and the status-quo, anti-communist side is readily seen in U.S. policy toward Latin America. On the one hand, the United States has put forth Franklin D. Roosevelt's Good Neighbor Policy, John F. Kennedy's Alliance for Progress, and Jimmy Carter's human rights policy and his attempts to deal constructively with the Nicaraguan revolution. On the other hand, Washington has supported the overthrow of elected governments in Guatemala and Chile, sponsored an invasion of Cuba, and directly invaded the Dominican Republic and Grenada.

The timing and extent of the swings between these two poles are essentially governed by U.S. domestic politics. Americans want their country to be strong and to prevent "communist expansion" in the Third World, but they do not want to fight wars to accomplish that. It has been a fundamental verity of domestic politics during the cold-war period that an administration must not "lose" a country to "communism" on its "watch"—especially a country in "our backyard." But since the Vietnam War, it has also been fundamental that Americans do not want to get involved in another long, costly war. These conflicting principles have created a dynamic in American foreign policy that has left U.S. allies confused. When a president tries to accommodate to change, he is criticized for being weak and soft on communism. When a president tries to stop change, he is criticized for being willing to get the country into war. So, Americans bounce back and forth, the victims of a contradictory attitude toward change and an inability to achieve a political consensus on how they can best serve their own interests in a changing world.

This dynamic is evident in recent American foreign policy. During the two decades following World War II, cold-war anti-communism was generally on the ascendancy. Any communist-dominated revolution was viewed as the equivalent of Soviet aggression, to be resisted at any cost lest the Soviet empire be further expanded.

During the trauma of Vietnam, the contradictions in this policy became apparent. Gradually, during the Vietnam years, the pendulum swung in the other direction. By the mid-1970s, the United States had entered a period when its revolutionary heritage was dominant. It actually elected a President who spoke of the nation's "inordinate fear of communism"—a phrase that would have been unthinkable for an American president to utter during the preceding 30 years. The Carter Administration intended to permit and even encourage change in the Third World.

But the United States did not really have the courage to let the process of change take its course. It discovered it could not control the process, and that made it uncomfortable. The United States gave them an inch, and they took a mile. Things happened that Americans did not like, and people wondered why Washington did not seem to be doing anything about it. Those who more strongly reflected the anti-communist, pro-stability side of the American character began to attack U.S. policies for being weak and vacillating. Eventually it became clear that the United States lacked a domestic consensus strong enough to enable it to carry out a policy of accommodation to change, particularly revolutionary change. Even before the Carter Administration was over, the United States began to swing back toward the anti-communist side.

The election of Ronald Reagan completed that swing. It ushered in an Administration with a rigidly bipolar view of the world, an Administration nostalgic for the days—if they ever existed—when American control and resolve were unquestioned, when Americans had friends and enemies but didn't have to bother about "third worldism." But if the United States lacks the domestic consensus necessary to support a policy of accommodation to change, its experience with Ronald Reagan makes it clear that there is even less of a consensus behind a policy of turning back the clock. If Americans lack the courage and self-confidence to live with change, even less do they have the courage and self-confidence to stop it. The longer the Reagan policies prevail, the clearer their costs will become. It is predictable that the pendulum will swing back again.

Central America is only the most current and most dramatic example of the continuing failure of the United States to come to terms with its experience in Vietnam and with the implications of that experience for its international role. I find the application of the Vietnam analogy to Central America unhelpful, but the degree to which the analogy drives the U.S. domestic debate is striking. On the one side, the Administration pursues a hard-line policy in Central America for the avowed purpose of demonstrating that the United States is once again strong and determined and is not going to "cut and run" in the face of "communist aggression" as it supposedly did in Vietnam and a lot of other places since. On the other side, many of the critics see the United States repeating in Central America the mistake it made in Vietnam of failing to understand and adjust to indigenous revolution. The one side passionately believes that the United States must once again demonstrate strength, but it believes that Americans must do so in ways that the other side believes, with equal passion, are wrong. Until Americans manage to achieve a new consensus on how the United States can act with strength and pride in a post-Vietnam world, polarization will continue, and international situations that evoke the Vietnam analogy will continue to be dealt with in a manner that dismays U.S. allies.

Concommitant with the breakdown of a foreign policy consensus in the United States as a result of the Vietnam War has been the greater entry of foreign policy issues into the arena of electoral politics. And because of that, successive administrations have, more than in the past, sought to distance themselves from the foreign policies of their predecessors. The Reagan Administration has exacerbated this phenomenon—and this will, predictably, cause an equally great reaction in its successor.

From my experience I have concluded that those principally responsible for Central America policy in the Reagan Administration have little patience with traditions like bipartianship and consultation with Congress and little interest in forging a bipartisan consensus with respect to Central America. The Administration's posture toward the Democratic opposition in Congress continues to be: we will pursue our policy in our way—and if we fail, we will blame *you* for losing Central America. Until the Republican Party is once again controlled by moderate, centrist elements capable and desirous of reaching accommodations with their counterparts in the Democratic Party on the basis of some minimally shared conceptions of what the world is like and where U.S. interests lie, I cannot hold out to our European friends much hope that the cacophony of voices struggling to control U.S. foreign policy will be stilled.

However, the approach I have advocated could, I believe, with sufficiently courageous leadership, gain the support of American public opinion, which is the sine qua non of a consistent, coherent policy. The Carter style failed to do this because it was perceived as weak and vacillating. The Reagan policies have clearly divided the American people. What is needed is a policy of the responsible use of strength—a policy that promotes U.S. interests without either taking on the role of the region's policeman or just letting events run their course.

Conclusion

Central America points up the importance of devising a better U.S. approach to the problems of political instability and revolutionary change in the Third World. To make such an approach possible, the United States' first problem is to convince itself that that is what its problem is. So long as Americans continue to view Central America as "theirs"—and therefore, by definition, as something apart from the Third World—they will continue to fight what will ultimately be losing battles, at increasing cost, against changes that are going to happen anyway. If Central America is a test, it is a test of the United States' ability to act with maturity, restraint, and a sense of proportion in responding to the region's dynamics.

But revolutions seem to rigidify U.S. policy. At the very time that flexibility is needed the most, the United States is at its most rigid. Because of Central America's geographic closeness and the United States' historically proprietary feelings toward the region, these rigidities are exacerbated with respect to that region. The United States has no strategy for dealing with political instability and revolutionary change there. Instead it attaches pejorative labels to phenomena as a substitute for dealing with them. Washington excuses itself from dealing with instability by labeling it "communist aggression" or "exporting revolution." It excuses itself from dealing with leftist governments and movements by labeling them "Marxist-Leninist" or "totalitarian." It excuses itself from negotiating by labeling it power sharing. The concept of negotiating to achieve a modus vivendi becomes alien to Americans. They become willing to negotiate only the non-negotiable, or to negotiate only after preconditions have been fulfilled that should themselves be the subject of the negotiations.

The more events move beyond U.S. control, the more stridently the United States insists on its vital interest in controlling them. Not knowing what else to do, Washington pours in ever more military aid. When Congress balks at providing more aid in the absence of a policy, the Reagan Administration threatens to accuse Congress of losing Central America if the aid is not forthcoming. Up go the interests; up go the stakes. This scenario is repeated several times a year. Washington becomes ever more locked in, ever more inflexible, ever more committed to the achievement of outcomes that are either unachievable or achievable only at costs that it has not yet told the public it will have to pay.

This whole syndrome of inflexible behavior reflects the absence of policy, of strategy, of thought. It reflects the inability of the

United States to cope—its incapacity to treat revolutionary phenomena with the sophistication that is required. It leads the United
States into a vicious cycle where the ways in which it responds to
change magnify the problems that change creates.

The United States must learn that the principal problem it faces
when it confronts revolutionary change in this region is neither the
Cubans nor the Soviets. The problem is learning how to be sensitive to developments in societies that lead them in the direction of
revolution, and how to respond to those changes in appropriate
ways in order to forestall reaching a point in the society where
revolution is the only option left. If the United States can do that,
containment of the Cubans and the Soviets in Central America
will be much easier.

The domino theorists on the left and the right are both wrong.
Central America is not inevitably going to fall to a Cuban-Soviet-
led, Marxist-Leninist revolutionary wave—unless the United
States persists in acting on the assumption that such a wave exists
and behaving in ways that nurture it. Paradoxically, the best way
to promote U.S. interests in Central America is to let go of it—not
in the isolationist sense of withdrawing from the region and failing
to use influence, but in the sense of turning the actors loose to seek
their own settlements with each other, with the United States playing an active and supportive role. If Washington insists on looking
at Central America as a region that is solely an arena of superpower competition, that must be either ours or theirs, it increases
the risk that those two choices will eventually obtain.

But the United States has been unable to cut loose because of
the inflexibility that has been imposed upon it by domestic political constraints. It should worry less about the communists wanting
to liberate Central America, and more about liberating itself from
the straitjacket of outmoded assumptions and policies that misun-
derstand—and therefore exacerbate—its problems in dealing with
political instability and revolutionary change in the Third World.

*This chapter has benefited from my association with a great many knowl-
edgeable people over the years. They are too numerous to mention, but
former U.S. Ambassadors Lawrence Pezzullo and Viron Vaky, especially,
will see many of their ideas in this chapter. My debt to Ambassador Vaky*

is obvious from a reading of his "Reagan's Central America Policy: An Isthmus Restored," in Robert S. Leiken's (ed.), Central America: Anatomy of Conflict. Robert Leiken and Richard Feinberg, to name just two others, have made valuable contributions, both through their writing and through their testimony before the Subcommittee on Western Hemisphere Affairs. I wish to thank the above-mentioned people, and also Robert Dockery, Richard Nuccio and Robert Kurz, for their very helpful comments on drafts of this chapter, and Nancy Agris for assistance with research. In particular, I wish to thank Victor C. Johnson, Staff Director of the Subcommittee on Western Hemisphere Affairs, for his invaluable assistance in the preparation of this chapter.

Alois Mertes

Europe's Role in Central America: A West German Christian Democratic View

Although Central America has been undergoing a process of social ferment and political instability for decades, it was only in the late 1970s, with the outbreak of civil war in El Salvador and the revolution against the dictatorship of Anastasio Somoza Debayle in Nicaragua, that the Western public suddenly became fully aware of the situation. This interest has been heightened by Soviet and Cuban attempts to exploit the situation in Central America in order to promote the long-term expansion of Soviet-controlled communist parties and by Moscow's and Havana's use of military intimidation to achieve that end. In recent years, European critics of nuclear deterrence have also been critics of the United States' Central America policy and supporters of the Sandinistas and the Salvadoran guerrillas. Despite its influence in the media, however, this group represents a minority, at least in the Federal Republic of Germany.

Central America's strategic location as a bridge between the North and South American continents, as well as between the Atlantic and the Pacific Oceans makes the United States particularly sensitive to developments in this region. Not only in Europe, but also in the United States, there is no uniform assessment on how best to deal with the economic, social and political developments in Central America. (There are as well aspects—such as demographics and the problems arising therefrom—which, while highly relevant, still receive little attention.)

The subject is also one of controversy within the European democracies, not only because of the pluralistic nature of public opinion-forming in our open societies, but also because assessments are made according to varying national experiences and political philosophies. Many misunderstandings in the European-

American relationship—and I am thinking here not so much of the governments as of the mass media and the parliaments—arise as a result of several differences: the geographic and geopolitical situation, the assessment of Soviet intentions, the distribution of power and responsibility within the alliance and worldwide, and, last but not least, the domestic political "moods" in the United States and the various countries of Europe.

Also, nothing is more essential than a dialogue of trust and confidence and as much consultation and collaboration between Europe and the United States as possible. I am convinced that we are not faced here with developments that must inevitably run counter to the interests of the United States and the Western world. Rather we have a good chance of preventing the crisis from ending in a political catastrophe (not to mention an international military conflict) and of bringing about peace, freedom, and justice—that is, basic human rights. A policy that is obliged to function under the pressure of events must of necessity take a clear position. There are questions that must be addressed in frank domestic and foreign policy discussions and above all between the North Atlantic Treaty Organization (NATO) partners. A requisite for a meaningful trans-Atlantic dialogue is readiness among all participants to learn and make adjustments. Accordingly, I will attempt in this essay to emphasize the points of view that are particularly important to the Christian-Democratic and conservative segments in Europe.

A significant difficulty for Europeans lies in the fact that unfortunately in the United States no broad consensus exists with regard to Latin America as one does, for example, with respect to the Berlin question or the issue of the U.S. military presence in Europe. There are also noteworthy differences in emphasis even within the Reagan Administration. Nonetheless, the American public has so far, despite the internal discussion in the United States itself, reacted with resentment to diverging European views on Central America. The Europeans are often collectively rebuked for false moralizing and legalism in their foreign policy toward Central America. There are those in Europe, however, who—just as the Democrats in Washington—accuse the U.S. government of pursuing an interventionist policy without regard to the rights of the peoples of the region or its historical and social development.

On September 28–29, 1984, in San José, Costa Rica, there was a meeting of the foreign ministers of Costa Rica, Guatemala, Honduras, El Salvador and Nicaragua; the Contadora Group of nations (Mexico, Colombia, Venezuela and Panama); and the ten member-states of the European Economic Community (EEC) as well as its two candidate-member countries, Spain and Portugal (see appendix).

Europeans and Central Americans once again thought of each other when faced with the common historical challenge of securing peace. It is no secret that the Foreign Minister of the Federal Republic of Germany (F.R.G.), Hans Dietrich Genscher, took the initiative for the San José conference. On October 4, 1984, he said in the Bundestag:

> Exactly because it is a matter of securing and maintaining—by peaceful means—economic stabilization, social justice, national sovereignty, and social pluralism in a geostrategically important region ridden by crises and conflicts, our friends in Central America need the partnership of the European Community. If we refuse this partnership, or if we are too fainthearted or even only too indecisive in our political and economic involvement, we will be abandoning the peoples of this region to growing destabilization and the burden of severe social problems. We are faced with the danger that Central America will become the arena of a heightened East-West conflict. We know that the United States of America agrees with us in this judgment.[1]

Third World—A Misleading Designation

Central America is a case *sui generis*. It would be only partially correct to say that this area of Latin America belongs to the "Third World," for in fact this designation applies to a thoroughly different reality that is highly disparate politically, economically and culturally. It would be more accurate to use the concept "non-aligned states" (in German the expression is "bloc-free states") when referring to Central America, as this emphasizes the fact of not belonging to any "bloc" such as the Warsaw Pact or the Atlantic Alliance. But since two of the Soviet Union's close strategic partners, namely Council of Mutual Economic Assistance members Cuba and Vietnam, are also counted among the nonaligned nations, it is important to differentiate between genuine nonalign-

---

[1] *Stenographischer Bericht*, 88th Session, p. 6426D.

ment and deceptive nonalignment. This substantial difference plays a central role in the case of Nicaragua. For nonalignment was one of the Sandinistas' most important promises. The West, as well as the Contadora Group and the rest of South America, want no more and no less than a genuine nonalignment of Central America as a precondition for a lasting solution that will bring peace, democracy, and social and economic progress to this region. Within the Third World, Latin America is distinguished by a unique characteristic: the European cultures of Spain and Portugal gave this part of the world its decisive stamp. First of all there is the language, which plays a large part in the formulation of thoughts and emotions. Then, too, there is Christianity, which in turn forms the basis of Europe's and America's law-based culture. Neither totalitarian rule nor economic exploitation of human beings is compatible with this ethos. And this jointly-shared ethos—more than simply the circumstance of belonging geographically to the Western Hemisphere—makes Latin America a zone of Western culture.

Indicative of this is the fact that in the United Nations, the Latin American states are the ones whose criteria most closely coincide with the values of Western nations on the question of human rights. It is counterproductive to try to reduce the psychological differences between South and North America by allocating fault; in many respects, these differences are a reflection of the former differences between Latin (Southern) Europe and Northern Europe. Particularly in light of their historical and psychological experiences, the participation of the Europeans, especially the EEC nations, can only be helpful in establishing peace in Central America.

Central America—A Special Case in the North-South Dialogue

Central America is certainly an example of the North-South relationship in the sense that it provides an antithetical contrast—i.e., industrialized countries versus developing nations. Hardly anyone will disagree that inadequate economic development is a decisive—historically, even the original—cause of the political crisis in Central America. The region consists, if Costa Rica is disregarded,

of a number of small developing countries whose political matura-
tion and movement toward democracy is inseparable from their
overcoming of unjust economic structures and social deprivation.
At the same time, Central America is in many respects surely a
special case within the Latin American component of the Third
World.

For some time the somewhat simplistic concept of the North-
South dialogue has been forming. The aim of this dialogue is to
overcome the economic gap between the industrialized nations of
the "North" and the developing countries of the "South." The
Soviet Union and its European allies theoretically belong to the
North. In fact, however, the developing countries see the North as
consisting of only the Western industrialized nations, in particular
North America, Western Europe and Japan.

The Soviet Union, for the most part, participates in the North-
South dialogue (especially within the framework of the United
Nations) with rhetoric and propaganda only. It points to its "spot-
less anticolonialist past" and commended itself—until its considerably successful invasion of Afghanistan in December 1979—to the
developing countries as their "natural ally." The active political, as
well as military, support of "national liberation movements" in
Asia, Africa and Latin America is among the most important pos-
tulates of Leninist foreign policy, to which all members of the
collective leadership and political bureaucracy in Moscow adhere
to this day.

This explains the standard "aid" given by the Soviet Union and
its allies to the developing countries: weapons; military advisers;
ideological, agitational, and organizational training. One can accuse the Soviet leaders of many things but not of making a secret
of the criteria for and goals of their international policy, particularly with respect to all varieties of national liberation movements.
Their plans are not kept locked away in some secret safe in the
Kremlin; rather, they are clearly manifest. Yet there are many
responsible people in the West—politicians, journalists, scientists,
even men of the church—who prefer, either from spiritual inertia
or out of fear of the consequences, to close their eyes and ears
rather than face reality: the Soviet Union has an antagonistic and
Manichaean view of history, in which only two worlds exist in the
final analysis. They are the intrinsically benevolent world of "real

socialism" (Soviet-style) that will bring about the ultimate good, and the intrinsically bad world of capitalism that conducts itself *contra salutem*. What in the West is considered rhetorical exaggeration (e.g., the Soviet Union as the evil empire) is, conversely, put forward in the Soviet Union as official doctrine regarding the West.

According to this conception, there is a battle "objectively" taking place between both worlds in which the socialist camp, under the leadership of the U.S.S.R., must of historical necessity win in the long run—and it must do so *without* a great war between East and West. This dynamic theory allows its practitioners many possibilities for pragmatic adaptation, for maneuvering according to circumstances, and for occasionally cooperating with the West, when it suits the exigencies of Soviet foreign policy. It is designed to always guarantee the preeminence of the static and dynamic security interests of the Soviet Union without harming the grand design of "peace through real socialism." Each step, no matter how small or slow, must be in "the right direction."

The Soviet Union evidently sees little sense in supporting a policy of evolutionary reforms. Therefore, the developing countries understand that the North in the North-South dialogue is, de facto, the West alone, because only the West is prepared to supply concrete development assistance to any relevant degree. Two facts are illustrative of this: (1) the Federal Republic of Germany gives more aid to the developing countries than the entire Soviet bloc put together; and (2) the EEC is by far the largest supplier of development assistance in the world—it provides more than half of the total development aid given by the West.

Central America—An Arena of East-West Rivalry

Central America has thus become a very significant example of East-West tension. This is the major reason why Central America, and particularly Nicaragua and El Salvador, have become an important political issue in Europe in recent years. The conduct of the United States, and especially its allegedly reactionary aims, was used by the "peace movement" and, unfortunately, also by a number of Social Democrats, as an argument against the deployment of U.S. intermediate-range nuclear missiles in Europe—and even against the NATO Alliance in general. Central America has become more and more a focus of the tensions between East and West as a result of the politically destabilizing role of Cuba and, *mutatis mutandis*, of Nicaragua, whose political and military dynamic is encouraged by the Soviet Union. At a Council on Mutual Economic Assistance meeting in Havana on October 30, 1984, Willi Stoph, Prime Minister of the German Democratic Republic (GDR), pledged to the Sandinistas "the firm and unshakable solidarity of the Socialist Unity Party and the government of the GDR" and announced "further measures to support the struggle of the Nicaraguan people";[2] this is language that hardly needs interpretation. We Germans know who built the most inhuman border system in the world through our country, who erected the Berlin Wall, and who is suppressing basic human, political and social rights in the GDR and Eastern Europe.

However, the men who govern and plan in Moscow are neither adventurers nor are they suicidal; rather, they are disciplined calculators, who in the interest of survival certainly do not want a military confrontation with the United States. The Soviet Union's Latin America policy is therefore extremely cautious, yet nonetheless purposeful in its long-term building of options for political influence, as has been demonstrated by its use of Cuba and Nicaragua to put pressure on the political systems of El Salvador, Honduras, Guatemala and Costa Rica, as well as on those of the small Caribbean island nations.

It is somewhat irrelevant for policymakers to ask which aspect of the Central American case—North-South or East-West—is of greater importance. Whether in the United States or Europe, those who neglect either one of these aspects are on the wrong path: they disregard the legitimate concerns of the peoples in question; hinder the genuine nonalignment of Central America; and abet the Soviet Union's global strategy to the long-term detriment of the United States and Western Europe, as well as the rest of Latin America. It seems to me that with respect to the Central American case, the European socialist parties differ from the conservative, Christian Democratic, and (in the European sense) liberal parties in the same way that their answers diverge on two fundamental

---

[2] *DDR-Spiegel*, Bonn: Press and Information Office, Federal Foreign Office, 1984.

questions relating to disarmament and security in Europe: (1) Is Soviet foreign policy pursuing static-defensive or dynamic-expansionist aims?; and (2) How concerned should the West be about the Soviet buildup of its military capabilities and its quest for political allies outside its own sphere of influence?

Opinions, whether on the subject of Central America, the debate regarding NATO's dual-track decision, or even on NATO strategy in general, divide according to how one approaches the questions mentioned above. Even within the same party, the F.R.G.'s former Chancellors Helmut Schmidt and Willy Brandt took opposite points of view on this, and the latter won out. The participation of Brandt (in his role as President of the Socialist International) in pacifist demonstrations against the nuclear-weapons deployments in the Federal Republic; and his comparison (at a pro-Sandinista demonstration on the eve of the November 1984 Nicaraguan elections) of U.S. policy toward Nicaragua with the Soviet aggression in Afghanistan; as well as his ostentatious display of friendship (using the intimate form of address) with President Fidel Castro during his October 1984 visit to Cuba, are the logical results of Brandt's inadequate assessment of Moscow's and Havana's strategy.

I respect the opinion of the leader of the Social Democratic Party (SPD). But it cannot be reconciled with what my political friends and I, to the best of our knowledge and conscience, consider to be essential in order to *preserve* peace with maximum reliability and to *shape*, short of risking war, an international environment that, step by step, will put a real and lasting end to all human oppression and exploitation. To go from the "frying pan" of an unsatisfactory situation into the "fire" of an even worse situation is not progress, but regression. It is the misfortune and tragedy of political responsibility that often there is no other choice than that between the lesser and the greater evil.

Central America—A Test for the Political Cohesion of the Atlantic Alliance

In contrast to the Warsaw Pact, NATO is not a compulsory military organization. It is a voluntary political alliance of constitutional democracies (Turkey being a special case) that have been threatened by a politically motivated, militarily powerful opponent ever since the subjugation of Eastern and Central Europe, with the formation of the Soviet Occupation Zone in Germany in 1945 and the first Soviet action against Berlin in 1948. The Soviet threat is political in nature, but military might has always had an essential role therein. Since Lenin, all communists have been Clausewitzians: political goals are paramount. The Soviets justify their challenge to the West, whether in Europe or Latin America, by saying they are carrying out an inevitable law of history. The challenge remains; in many respects it is even growing; it is patient and tough; it takes its time. The Soviets feel encouraged by hostile tendencies in Western Europe toward NATO, by neoisolationists in the United States, by complications in the Middle East and by the crisis in Central America. Moscow's political behavior is aided by the tendency of the West to lock itself "pragmatically" into the category of the "foreseeable future" and to dismiss everything beyond that as nonexistent—as theoretical speculation irrelevant to current policy. The phrase, "Vigilance is the price of freedom," remains as valid as ever. It is valid in regard to the long-term goals of Cuba and the Soviet Union in Central America. Western Europe and North America view Moscow's political goals and military potential as a threat to their independence and freedom.

Soviet global policy is determined by two clearly recognizable impulses:

— an insatiable notion of security, which views the free trade unions in Poland, the Dubček reforms in Czechoslovakia, the desire for freedom of the entire German people, and the common defense determination of Western Europe and the United States as threats; and

— a global-revolution ideology, which asserts that the world must become communist in order to be peaceful and just. Whether or not Soviet foreign policymakers are true believers in communism is of little relevance for they believe that "proletarian internationalism" and "active solidarity" with countries like Nicaragua and with guerrillas like those in El Salvador are the important instruments in furthering Soviet influence and expanding Soviet power.

In contrast to the accepted Western concept of security, which in essence means military defense, the Soviet concept of security is of a comprehensive political nature. Military might—i.e., growing options for intimidating and threatening the outside world—remains the Soviet political leadership's decisive instrument. The offensive aspects of the Soviet security concept are: iron control of the "cordon sanitaire" in Europe; the disciplining (i.e., the suppression) of political opponents in the Soviet camp; and the unceasing attempt to discredit the United States in Europe, be it as an unreliable ally or as a dangerous global adventurer. In this way the two sides of the trans-Atlantic community are to be set against one another and the strategy of deterrence is to be politically undermined. Parallel to this is the Soviet continuation of threats and offensive political intimidation of West European democratic states, the ultimate aim of which is to force the West to give in to pressure and blackmail should a real confrontation arise. After all, the West philosophizes over the alternative "better red than dead" in peacetime and thereby suggests a stance of political appeasement.

Ultimately it is not the territory of the Federal Republic of Germany that the Soviet Union wants to conquer, but rather the minds and hearts of its people, especially the younger generation, who know only from older generations and from books about Hitler and appeasement, about Stalin and Khrushchev, about the two Berlin crises, and the importance of the United States to the Federal Republic's vital interests. Added to this is the fact that in the period of U.S.-Soviet nuclear bilateralism (the Test Ban Treaty, Nonproliferation Treaty, SALT I, SALT II) and détente in the 1970s (Bonn's *Ostpolitik*, the Helsinki Final Acts), public understanding and awareness of the nature and intensity of the Soviet threat receded significantly. The Federal Republic's Chancellor Helmut Kohl characterized the nature of this threat when he said: "Moscow wants a political victory with an atomic peace."

Those in the West who are realistic enough to call attention to this truth are accused by many in Europe and the United States of being cold warriors, captives of the "enemy as depicted." This is wrong; such realism is the prerequisite both for the West's defensive security *from* the Soviet Union and for its collaborative security (through arms control and disarmament) *with* the Soviet Union.

Such realism is also the best argument for Western Europe's

solidarity with the United States regarding Central America. The argument that "the Americans display solidarity with the Europeans on security issues in the face of the Soviet threat to Western Europe, therefore the Europeans must display solidarity vis-à-vis the Soviet threat to the United States in Central America" is a false parallel and should not be the primary reason for European support of the United States. Of course Europe should demonstrate solidarity with Washington in dealing with the problems of Central America. But this issue should not be allowed to jeopardize the cohesion of the NATO Alliance.

The credibility of NATO's strategy, especially the U.S. nuclear guarantee for Europe, is based on a premise that today is forgotten by many pacifists in Europe and several neoisolationists in the United States: the security of the Alliance is indivisible because there is only one single threat. The credibility of the U.S. nuclear shield for Europe, which for nearly 40 years has guaranteed peace with freedom, is based—particularly in the eyes of the Soviet leadership—on the fact that these guarantees arise from the United States' vital interest in preventing Western Europe from becoming dependent on Moscow. Whoever portrays these guarantees as merely an act of American altruism toward the Europeans destroys their credibility in the eyes of the Soviets and the Europeans. Every form of American isolationism results in promoting Soviet psychological expansion into Western Europe. The same is true in reverse: Europe's essential solidarity with the United States is an act of self-preservation. Every manifestation of anti-Americanism in Europe, in failing to recognize the basic mutuality of the interests of the Western democracies and thereby weakening the trans-Atlantic relationship, is a boon to Soviet diplomacy.

The 1962 Cuban missile crisis made clear to Europe that a crisis of the security of the Western Hemisphere has direct repercussions for Europe. Until now, the Soviet Union has not viewed Latin America—with the exception of Cuba, which is a special case—as a region in which it has special interests. But it lies within the logic of the Soviet Union's efforts to discredit and weaken the United States in Europe, the Middle East, and Latin America, as well as in Soviet ideological pretensions to systematically exploit every instability and crisis outside its own sphere of influence. In Central America it is obviously pursuing the goal of promoting sources of unrest on the U.S. southern flank. While Soviet actions in the region avoid a direct military provocation against the security of the United States, they are still politically virulent enough to divert U.S. vigilance away from Europe. A dissipation of U.S. strength with regard to Central America, combined with an intensification of the Central American debate within the United States itself, would be very convenient to the Soviet Union. The U.S.S.R. is interested in seeing an increase in isolationist sentiments in the United States, for this would allow the Soviets more political maneuverability in Europe and the Middle East, which could eventually lead to a decrease in the political resolve and strategic credibility of the United States. Nevertheless, I am convinced that the Soviet Union is not seeking a real confrontation with the United States in Central America, at least not in the foreseeable future. Cuba knows this, too, and so do the Sandinistas.

Cuba, as a Latin American country, plays a somewhat different role in the region than does the Soviet Union. Castro feels pledged to revolution in Latin America more directly and more ideologically than the Soviet leadership, which subordinates the concept of world revolution to its own global imperialist interests. Since the October 1983 intervention by the United States and the East Caribbean states in Grenada, however, Cuba has again become more acutely aware of its precarious geographical location. It announced clearly to its Sandinista friends that ultimately Managua would not be able to count on military protection from Cuba. Nonetheless, Cuba has a massive number of military advisers and civilian personnel in Nicaragua, and is thereby party to the conflict in Central America. It is evident that the Cuban military presence in Nicaragua is intended to discourage and complicate any American contingency plans for an overt military intervention in Central America and to intimidate Nicaragua's militarily weak neighbors as well as to form the political and logistical base for the guerrillas in El Salvador.

The F.R.G.'s Political and Economic Relations with Central America

Of all the EEC countries, the Federal Republic of Germany maintains the closest economic ties with Central America. As a European state whose security depends on the credibility of the West's deterrence capability the Federal Republic can only do justice to its Alliance responsibilities by conducting an active policy toward Central America.

Among Europeans, Germans have taken a special interest in Latin America, at least since the time of Alexander von Humboldt's scientific explorations there in the early 1800s. Whereas the French and British focused most of their attention in the eighteenth century on dividing up Asia and Africa amongst themselves, the Germans became far more involved in Latin America, which was for them an open continent and a free market. Also, Germany's economic relations with Latin America, which were developed through private initiative, continue today. Throughout history political relations were considered so "problem-free" that the public was only vaguely aware of them.

Today, the Federal Republic is the most important EEC trading partner of the five nations that comprise the Central American Common Market (i.e., Costa Rica, El Salvador, Guatemala, Honduras and Nicaragua). In the first nine months of 1984, the Federal Republic of Germany exported 622 million deutsche marks (DM) worth of goods to these five countries and Panama; its imports over the same period came to DM727 million. (The F.R.G.'s balance of trade with Central America has traditionally been negative.) In addition, the Federal Republic alone accounts for more than ten percent of all the exports of several Central American countries.

German immigration has also been of great significance to many Latin American countries; there are approximately five million Latin Americans of German extraction. They have preserved their cultural and ethnic identity, while at the same time taking part in the economic, and gradually also in the political, development process. Because many are highly qualified technicians and businessmen, these immigrants have done much to enhance Germany's standing in Latin America. Also, in most countries there are German cultural centers and schools. Of the 114 schools abroad that receive staffing and financial support from the Federal Republic, 38 are in Latin America, and a number of these are in Central America. German cultural history has had a great influence on Latin America. Kant's philosophy was brought to the region via

Spain, and Hegel and Marx have found disciples in Latin America, as has the sociology of Max Weber.

Nor should one underestimate the relationship between many contemporary political parties in Latin America and their European counterparts, and in particular those from the F.R.G. The political foundations in the Federal Republic have gained a thorough knowledge of the economic and political problems of the region through their joint work with Latin American parties. I, as a Christian Democrat, am particulary gratified to see the formation of modern Christian Democratic parties in Central America, as in other parts of Latin America. Yet it would be unfair not to mention that the Social Democrats, too, have contributed much toward the modernization of the party system in Latin America.

The Federal Republic of Germany maintains diplomatic relations with all the countries of Central America. Although the Federal Republic's Ambassador to El Salvador was recalled to Bonn in the early 1980s for security reasons, the Federal Republic's embassy in San Salvador is once again fully staffed. Bilateral contacts with the countries of the region have continued to be strengthened on all levels in recent years.

Especially close today are the F.R.G.'s relations with *Costa Rica*, a country in whose political and social institutions the Federal Republic sees a model for the other Central American nations. This relationship has been further strengthened by the visits of Foreign Minister Genscher to San José in 1981, 1983 and 1984, and by the visit of Costa Rican President Luis Alberto Monge to the F.R.G. in June 1984. Costa Rica is also a focal point for the Federal Republic's collaboration on development policy in the region.

I place great hopes in the future development of the Federal Republic's relations with *El Salvador*. President José Napoleón Duarte's close personal contacts with the Christian Democratic Union (CDU) make it possible for Bonn to follow the political process in El Salvador particularly closely. (After assuming office, Duarte visited the F.R.G. in July 1984.) Also, during his September 1984 visit to San Salvador Jürgen Warnke, the Federal Republic's Minister for Economic Cooperation, agreed to provide El Salvador with DM50.6 million in economic aid within a framework of financial and technical cooperation. These monies are intended for the promotion of agricultural projects, housing, food production, professional training, and small and medium-sized enterprises. In the CDU's opinion, Duarte's socially responsible efforts to reform and modernize his country deserve complete support.

In the years just following the overthrow of Somoza, the Schmidt government gave generous support to the Sandinista regime in *Nicaragua*. This support was based on the hope that the junta would swiftly enact the goals it had proclaimed—pluralism, nonalignment, and a mixed economy. Reality, however, looks very different: those who bring Soviet and Cuban military advisers into their country and have their security forces trained by advisers from the GDR State Security Service have abandoned the path of genuine nonalignment. Pluralism in Nicaragua hardly exists any longer as a result of the Sandinistas' de facto sole rule over the state. Also, the Sandinistas seem to have abandoned the goal of a mixed economy.

Chancellor Kohl has resolved not to give any further bilateral state aid to Nicaragua as long as Managua continues to support the Salvadoran guerrillas in destabilizing that country. Because the government of the Federal Republic does not wish to renege on agreements, however, it will allow programs already in progress to be carried to their conclusion.

Honduras, too, is among those countries with which the Federal Republic cooperates in development policy. The stabilization of this, the poorest Central American country, surely deserves more attention than it has received to date.

Relations with *Guatemala* have been burdened by the particularly grievous human rights violations in that country in recent years. The constitutional assembly elections in the summer of 1984 and the announcement of presidential elections for 1985 raise some hope that conditions there will gradually improve. Guatemala's constructive role in the San José conference is also a positive factor that encourages expectations for the future.

Europe's Relations with Central America

The EEC is, after the United States, Central America's most important export market and its second-largest foreign investor. In 1982 the Central American nations exported approximately DM2.7 billion worth of goods to the EEC countries and imported from them goods worth approximately DM900 million. Also, for some years Central America has been the focal point of the EEC's assistance to Latin America. From 1979 to 1983 the EEC gave DM560 million in aid to Central America—predominantly financial and technical assistance, but also food aid.

At present, 85 percent of all imports from Latin America are admitted to the EEC tariff-free, or at a tariff of five percent or less. For those countries that are not linked to Europe by the 1975 Lomé Agreement between 64 developing African, Caribbean and Pacific countries and the EEC, the system of general preferential treatment was created. Since July 1971 it has provided full tariff exemptions on all Latin American industrial products and partial exemptions as well as partial reductions on a large portion of Latin America's agricultural and tropical processed goods. To date Latin Americans have not taken full advantage of this preferential treatment.

For a long time there was no uniform European policy toward Latin America. The European Political Cooperation of the EEC passed a major test when during the Falkland Islands/Malvinas crisis the European nations were called upon to demonstrate solidarity with Great Britain. As a result of this conflict, which interrupted traditional relations with the Argentinian people, the Europeans realized that they had to develop a more active Latin American policy.

The ten countries of the European Economic Community have sought a dialogue with Latin America in recent years. Closer cooperation was agreed upon in the Andean Pact, a non-preferential cooperation agreement made between the EEC nations and Bolivia, Colombia, Ecuador, Peru and Venezuela in December 1983. A dialogue will start with the La Plata Basin countries of Argentina, Uruguay, Paraguay and Bolivia, and contacts have been established between the Latin American Economic System and the EEC.

The Ten have found a great willingness in Latin America to intensify relations with Europe. At first the conflict in Central America led to differing assessments among the European governments. The 1981 French-Mexican declaration recognizing the Salvador rebels as a "representative political force" was judged critically by France's European partners. Over time, however, a stronger consensus developed among the ten EEC partners. It received its first binding expression in the June 1983 Stuttgart declaration of the Community's European Council:

> The Heads of State and Government confirmed their close interest in developments in Central America. They are deeply concerned at the economic and social conditions in many parts of the region, at the tensions which these create and at the widespread misery and bloodshed.
>
> They are convinced that the problems of Central America cannot be solved by military means, but only by a political solution springing from the region itself and respecting the principles of non-interference and inviolability of frontiers. They, therefore, fully support the current initiative of the Contadora Group. They underlined the need for the establishment of democratic conditions and for the strict observance of human rights throughout the region.
>
> They are ready to continue contributing to the further development in the area, in order to promote progress towards stability.[3]

The San José conference was a preliminary high point in Europe's efforts to contribute actively to regional conflict management and the guaranteeing of peace in Central America. The Central American nations again voiced their wish to diversify their external relations politically and economically. Europeans are convinced that this desire requires a response from the democratic states of Europe—that is, a response from countries that are friends and allies of the United States and therefore know that a real threat to U.S. security would have incalculable consequences for the security of Europe.

The EEC will commence talks as soon as possible with the states of Central America on a cooperation agreement that will provide for closer collaboration in the areas of trade and development assistance. This collaboration is aimed at combatting the deeper causes of the conflicts in Central America. These lie—and I repeat a truism—in economic backwardness, social injustice, and political tyranny. These factors have given rise to instability and have opened the region to the influence of revolutionaries. As President Reagan correctly said in a letter he wrote to Venezuela's citizens in 1982, "There are two fundamental causes for the conflict in Cen-

---

[3] See the *Bulletin of the European Communities Commission*, Vol. 16, No. 6, 1983, p. 23.

tral America: the economic, social and political underdevelopment and the forcible exploitation of this underdevelopment by Cuba, Nicaragua and the Soviet Union. In order to bring peace to this region, in our opinion, both causes must be eliminated."[4]

In 1985 the EEC will provide a total of 60 million European Currency Units—that is, some $50 million—in financial and technical assistance to Central America. With the customary five-year term of such cooperation agreements, this alone could channel some $250 million into the region.

Another goal of the collaboration between Europe and Central America is to further integration on the isthmus—something that has been stagnating for years. The San José conference showed that collaboration between the two regions can also promote a sense of Central American identity and draw out mutual bonds among those nations. The participation of future EEC members, Spain and Portugal, in this effort should make it possible to draw, in the economic sphere, on those historical ties that bind Spain to the region.

The European View of Developments in the Region

In speaking generally of "Central America," one must not fail to take into account the great differences between the individual countries of the isthmus. For example, the dependent conditions, dating from the Spanish colonial period, of the original Indian population in Guatemala cannot be compared to the social structures (marked by small agrarian enterprises) of the Costa Rican people, the great majority of whom are descended from Spaniards. El Salvador has always been economically more developed than its neighbor Honduras, which is among the poorest countries in Latin America.

The heritage of its past hangs heavily on Central America. Until only a short time ago, the traditional alliance between oligarchy

---

[4] "Letter to Venezuelans on World Peace and the Situation in Central America and the Caribbean, November 5, 1982," in *Public Papers of the Presidents of the United States*, Reagan Administration, 1982, Washington, D.C.: GPO, 1983, pp. 1433–35.

and military was still dominant. The great majority of the population continued to subsist in poverty and backwardness.

Common to all Central American countries is the dominating influence of the United States, which traditionally wielded power through the ruling oligarchies and more than once intervened in the region. The struggle for social and political change in Central America has therefore very often been accompanied by strong anti-Americanism. In a speech to the Organization of American States, in which he spoke of the common ideals of the peoples of the Western Hemisphere, President Reagan noted:

> We have not always lived up to these ideals; all of us at one time or another in our history have been politically weak, economically backward, socially unjust or unable to solve our problems through peaceful means. My own country, too, has suffered from internal strife including a tragic Civil War . . . and, yes, at times we have behaved arrogantly and impatiently toward our neighbors.
>
> These experiences have left their scars, but they also help us today to identify with the struggle for political and economic development in the other countries of this hemisphere.[5]

Since informed and responsible Americans realize and openly admit how significant a role the United States' past errors have played in the formation of Latin Americans' convictions and prejudices, I, as a European, see little sense in self-righteously joining in on reproaches and complaints about former U.S. generations. The politician of today must have knowledge of the past, but his task is to shape the future.

Economic and social problems, however, are not the only reasons for the tensions in Central America. It must not be forgotten, for example, that in the years from 1950 to 1970, Central America was among the regions of highest economic growth in the world. In countries such as El Salvador and Costa Rica, and Honduras and Nicaragua as well, the economic dynamic led to an unusually high degree of social mobility. This in no way fits into the picture of an ossified social structure that predominates in the minds of many Europeans.

The one-sided ownership structure in rural areas eventually led

---

[5] See *The New York Times*, February 25, 1982, p. A14.

to the formation of a modern agrarian sector in Central America. But urban industry and the service enterprises could absorb neither the workers freed from the land nor the rapidly growing population. While the country was modernizing, misery was growing, and with it, social tensions. The traditional political system was inflexible in the face of these developments. The striving of the old oligarchies to preserve their power caused severe political polarization in Central America.

As in the other Latin American nations, young reformers in Central America, primarily of Christian Democratic and Social Democratic alignment, have pushed their way into the political arena in recent years. In domestic policy they stand for "revolution in freedom," to wit, the program of the Christian Democratic parties of Latin America, which calls for land reform, social democracy and political pluralism. In foreign policy the reformers strive for greater freedom of movement. They seek a certain distancing from the United States in order to safeguard the internal legitimation of their respective governments in the face of latent anti-U.S. sentiments. These forces work closely with their European sister parties.

In the dialogue between the Christian Democrats of Europe and Latin America, the theme "equidistance from both superpowers" plays an important role. The CDU and Christian Social Union have attempted to show their friends in Latin America how unacceptable it is for them to equate the U.S.S.R. and the United States. While the Soviet Union tried twice to undermine the freedom of Berlin and suppressed all political and trade-union freedoms in its sphere of influence, the United States has for decades proved itself to be a reliable guarantor of the freedom of West Berlin, the Federal Republic of Germany and Western Europe. Christian Democrats and liberals in the F.R.G. consider it wholly inappropriate to place the constitutionally democratic United States on a par with the totalitarian U.S.S.R. At the same time, prominent Latin American politicians have said to me: particularly in Central America, we urgently need the United States—not only its economic strength, but also its deterrence capability to guard against all expansionist incursions. Grenada was therefore an indispensable action, and it proved to be a success.

But, as these same persons emphasize, to say this openly would be detrimental to them domestically. It seems to me that this "dual language" is a problem that places a special burden on the relationship between Latin and North America.

The Situation in El Salvador and Nicaragua

Until the late 1970s, Marxist-Leninist revolutionaries supported the reform-oriented forces in Central America. This coalition of opponents of the old order began to disintegrate after the Sandinistas' victory over Somoza in Nicaragua, when it became clear that the Marxists were not prepared to make compromises with the reformers. In El Salvador in early 1980 the Social Democrats and the Marxists left the reform-oriented junta that had overthrown General Carlos Humberto Romero Mena in 1979. The Christian Democrats remained in the junta, a decision which, in the face of the increasing terror from the right, confronted the party with a severe test.

The incipient civil war in El Salvador was marked by the uncompromising stance both of the extreme right and the extreme left. The human rights violations by the military and the death squads damaged El Salvador's international standing, while early on the guerrillas met with sympathy from segments of the rural population. This changed after the reform-oriented Christian Democrats under Duarte offered an alternative. Duarte's program was: land reform, elections, economic reconstruction, and the combatting of terrorism of both the right and the left.

The 1984 elections, which have now made Duarte the legitimately elected president of El Salvador, demonstrated that the majority of the population supports reform. With the help of the United States, Duarte was able to strengthen his authority over the military. This made it possible to begin a dialogue with the insurgents from a position of legitimacy and strength. Duarte's talks with the guerrillas in La Palma in late 1984 demonstrated his desire for peace. He can continue to count on the support of the European Christian Democrats in this pursuit.

In Nicaragua, even before the "contras" took up arms against the Sandinistas, the government in Managua, with the help of Moscow and Havana, began a massive arms buildup unlike anything in neighboring countries. An observation made in 1976 by the GDR's Minister of Defense, Heinz Hoffmann, helps to explain why this tactic is being pursued: "What role does military force play in the victory or defeat of a revolution in the epoch of the transition from capitalism to socialism? Can such a revolution take place without a single shot being fired? Until now, indeed, history has not known a single case in which a socialist revolution was carried to victory without the cannons having spoken their word of power, or at least without their having been aimed and loaded."[6] Havana and Moscow and their European allies see the 4,000 military and security advisers they have in Nicaragua as serving to further the socialist revolution.

Despite generous economic and political support from Western Europe and the United States, the Sandinistas began to turn toward Moscow shortly after they assumed power, as was evidenced by the fact that as early as 1979 their party secured its relations with the Soviet Communist Party by means of a treaty. Under external military pressure, the already intractable domestic political situation hardened further. Europe and the United States increasingly restrained their support, and the economic situation in Nicaragua grew ever more precarious.

The elections on November 4, 1984, took place under tight Sandinista control and the opposition was given only a trifling amount of latitude. Confronted by incessant obstacles during the campaign, a large portion of the opposition felt unable to take part in the elections. Concessions by the Sandinistas came too late to offer a fair chance for political pluralism. Internal power struggles between Sandinista factions complicated the picture even more. Only a dialogue between the government and the opposition can, perhaps, offer a chance for the reversal of political developments that is so vital to peace and stability in Nicaragua.

Is the West's Credibility at Stake in Central America?

Credibility arises when claims and implementation converge, when rhetoric and concrete policy concur, and when those who

---

[6] See *Sozialistische Landesverteidigung*, German Democratic Republic, 1979.

ask for trust have the courage to stand up for their ideals and convictions.

The Western democracies are committed to pluralism and tolerance, to respect for the basic rights of the individual, to social justice, and to the transformation of traditional social structures by means of reforms. At the international level, they demand a peaceful resolution of conflicts, fair reconciliation of interests, and respect for the political sovereignty of other states. To the Western democracies, international law is the basis for the peaceful coexistence of nations. It provides civilized means for the arbitration and settlement of conflicts. In particular, it renounces both the use of threats and the use of force as a means to achieve political aims. It recognizes only one exception, and that is the individual and collective self-defense of nations.

The credibility of the West is at stake in Central America in a number of ways:

— The West must prove to Latin America that it does not primarily support the traditional power elites, but rather is prepared to stand up in the region for Western values such as democracy, the constitutional state, and social justice. The aims of Western policy must reflect these basic values. This requires tolerance and respect for the right of the Latin American peoples to find their own political path, no less than it requires readiness to support those forces that are fighting for democracy and reform. It would be a fatal signal, extending far beyond the confines of the region, if the West were to give the impression that it was deserting those who are fighting for the values for which the West stands. The West must prove that social change is possible with its support.

— The United States, as the leading Western power, can retain its credibility if, through a combination of prudent long-term diplomacy, economic assistance, and credible military deterrence, it prevents the Soviet Union from expanding its geostrategic sphere of influence to Latin America through the exploitation of internal conflicts. The West must make clear that it will not accept a substantial shift in the international balance in favor of the Soviet Union. Such a position embodies respect for genuine nonalignment but not the acceptance of the premise that the Soviet Union is a "natural ally" of the nonaligned in Central America.

The credibility of the leading Western power will remain intact if, while still preserving all necessary options, the United States subordinates military power to the primacy of politics in Central America—that is, if it continues to give top priority to the search for durable political solutions. This way Americans and Europeans can prove their common interest as Western democracies in a manner that does justice, not only to the short-term exigencies in Central America, but also to the long-term objectives of achieving peace, democracy, and economic and social progress in the region. The report of the National Bipartisan Commission on Central America (i.e., the Kissinger Commission) attempted to reflect this comprehensive approach.

— For the Europeans, the credibility of their political solidarity with the United States is at stake in Central America. Unlike in the Eastern bloc, in the Western Alliance there is an open and critical discussion about the policies of all its members. This includes the policies of its leading power, the United States, whose strategic credibility (including its option of nuclear first use) is crucial to Europe's security. In view of this, the United States must be able to expect that its European partners will not impute malevolence to their main ally in its policy toward Central America. Differing interpretations of the best methods to achieve the West's mutual goals should be discussed openly, but in a spirit of Atlantic solidarity, which, I repeat, is essential both to Americans and Europeans for the preservation of their common interests.

These are inseparable. It would be extremely unfortunate if we Europeans, while seeking a discourse between East and West, were incapable of pursuing an amicable dialogue with our chief ally. The decisive criterion for a dialogue among friends is their shared basic values, and this also holds true for Europe and the United States with respect to their Central America policy.

A common Western position on Central America based on free choice and mutual consultation and discussion would contribute to the strengthening of the West's credibility throughout the world. This would be particularly important for the younger generation in Europe, which no longer thinks the West has the ability or the strength to deal in common with dangerous conflicts like those in Central America, and which is especially critical of the United States. (The media's one-sided reports and commentaries on Central America, those of European television and radio in particular, contribute to this bias.)

— As for the West European countries, their own credibility is at stake in Central America (and in the rest of Latin America as well) with respect to their being able to make independent political and material contributions to the elimination of economic and social injustice. Purely verbal declarations by Europeans do not help; they only lead to embittering the North Americans, disappointing the Central Americans, and encouraging the Cubans and Soviets. The San José conference showed clearly that the Central Americans and the Contadora nations expect a concrete European contribution and that Europe is prepared to make one. This in no way alters the fact that the United States remains Central America's most important partner in every respect.

Europe's contribution should enable the Central American states to achieve the diversification they desire in their foreign policy and external economic relations. This aim can only remain credible if European policy is not perceived as merely a function of U.S. policy. An independent European contribution should not, however, be an obstacle to coordination on certain efforts, especially now that a large number of programs are already being carried out with the help of the United States within the framework of the inter-American system.

— Highest priority must be given to avoiding positions and situations that would leave the United States no alternative but that of either losing credibility as the leading Western power or of resorting to a military intervention. We Europeans, in the interest of the indivisibility of the security of all members of the Atlantic Alliance, must do everything possible to prevent our chief ally from being put in such a position. Were Central America to distract the United States psychologically, politically or militarily from the focal point of the Soviet threat and of Western security— namely Europe—the consequences for the cohesion of the Atlantic Alliance would be incalculable.

Is a European Contribution to the Stabilization of Central America Possible?

The goal of every Western country's Central America policy must be to bring about economic recovery, social improvements, and political stabilization. Progress on the road to democracy and as expeditious an implementation of constitutional conditions as possible are among the prerequisites for stabilization. But these goals are interdependent: economic recovery cannot take place without political stabilization, and social improvements must be supported by solid economic development.

It is the West's goal to bring about peaceful social change that will allow Central America to escape from the convulsions of war and civil war. It would be dangerous if in the long run the impression were to develop that the only alternative to repressive rightist regimes is Cuban- and Soviet-supported revolution and that the West will always automatically act in the interest of counter-revolution.

Revolutionaries tend to offer quick, patent solutions. These usually disappoint very quickly. Sound, durable reforms require time, though this does not suspend the social dynamic. The forces for reform in Central America, who display patience and resoluteness in the pursuit of their aims, should be encouraged, even if they cannot honestly promise quick results.

The San José conference showed that a European contribution to the stabilization of the region is possible and that the European countries are also prepared to make one. Not only the planned agreement on economic cooperation, but also, and above all, the agreement to conduct a political dialogue between Europe and Central America will be components of this.

In addition, the EEC nations and the European members of NATO will have to deepen their dialogue with Washington regarding the problems in Central America in order to determine the West's mutual interests in the region and the criteria for guiding Western policy. Only a unified European policy toward Central America can bring the necessary weight to bear on Washington in order to make an active contribution to peace and development in the region.

An important, specifically German contribution to European policy in Central America is the work of the foundations of four of the Federal Republic's major political parties—the CDU, CSU, SPD, and FDP (Free Democratic Party). These foundations try to find partners in Central American countries, particularly among political parties, trade unions and cooperatives. They also carry out projects financed by the Federal Ministry for Economic Cooperation. Their aim is to strengthen the parties at the center of the political spectrum in order to overcome the extreme polarization under which many Central American countries operate.

Only in Costa Rica are all four foundations active. The SPD's Friedrich Ebert Foundation works closely with the governing National Liberation Party, and the CDU's Konrad Adenauer Foundation works with the United Social Christian Party. The FDP's Friedrich Naumann Foundation supports the local editorial staffs of small radio stations in Costa Rica, and the CSU's Hanns Seidel Foundation supports an employers' institute.

In Nicaragua and Honduras, all the foundations are represented, with the exception of the Hanns Seidel Foundation. The Friedrich Ebert Foundation does not support any party in Managua but rather works with the Supreme Court, judicial administrative bodies, and the Ministry for Social Affairs and Education. The Konrad Adenauer Foundation supports the Social Christian Party and the Christian Democratic Federation of Trade Unions. The Friedrich Naumann Foundations's partner is the Independent Liberal Party, and the foundation provides financial support to the newspaper *La Prensa*.

In Guatemala only the Friedrich Naumann Foundation is still active after security considerations caused the Christian Democratic and Social Democratic foundations to recall their personnel. In El Salvador, the only foundation active is the Konrad Adenauer, which works closely with the governing Christian Democratic Party. The foundation and its Salvadoran partners have contributed significantly to the creation of democratic infrastructures throughout the country.

The European emphasis on NATO's not being active beyond its territorial boundaries is often reproached by Americans as European "legalism." But the founders of NATO consciously renounced establishing a global alliance. The political weight of the United States as a nuclear superpower and its accompanying responsibility differentiates it from the European countries, who are no longer in a position to take on worldwide commitments. This is also true in the military sphere for the Federal Republic of Germany, which at the joint urging of the United States and the Soviet Union pledged itself to a comprehensive renunciation of nuclear weapons. The establishment of a defined geographical NATO area freed the Alliance from burdens arising out of decolonization, as well as from the wars in the Near and Middle East and Vietnam. NATO was thereby able to confine itself to the area of its main task—i.e., Western Europe, which plays so decisive a role for the security of the West as a whole. The differing roles of Europe and the United States within the Atlantic Alliance need not, however, preclude an appropriate division of labor.

Two quotations should remind us that the United States and Canada, like the European members of NATO, have always seen their security interests as interdependent with the rest of the world. The 1967 Harmel Report on the Future Tasks of the Alliance, states that, "The North Atlantic Treaty area cannot be treated in isolation from the rest of the world. Crises and conflicts arising outside the area may impair its security either directly or by affecting the global balance."[7]

Fifteen years later, in their Bonn declaration, the heads of state of the NATO nations, reinforced the connection between development and security by saying:

> Our purpose is to contribute to peaceful progress worldwide; we will work to remove the causes of instability, such as under-development or tensions which encourage outside interference. We will continue to play our part in the struggle against hunger and poverty. Respect for genuine non-alignment is important for international stability. All of us have an interest in peace and security in other regions of the world. We will consult together as appropriate on events in these regions which may have implications for our security, taking into account our commonly identified objectives. Those of us who are in a position to do so will endeavour to respond to requests for assistance from sovereign states whose security and independence is threatened.[8]

How Can We Overcome the Misperceptions Among Americans and Europeans?

The current mutual reproaches between European and Americans are the result of a lack of understanding that stems from two sources:

---

[7] "The Future Tasks of the Alliance (Harmel Report)," Report of the Council, Annex to the Final Communiqué of the NATO Ministerial Meeting, Brussels, December 1967.
[8] "Declaration of the Heads of State and Government Participating in the Meeting of the North Atlantic Council at Bonn," NATO, Brussels, June 10, 1982, p. 3.

— differing assessments of the larger international determinants of the crisis in Central America;

— differing perceptions of the events in Central America itself.

Events such as the mining of Nicaraguan harbors with the help of the Central Intelligence Agency or the discovery of a CIA handbook for "white terror" create in Europe, especially among young people, the impression that the United States is enmeshed in sinister intrigues. As a European politician, I must look on this with consternation, because from such perceptions and the emotional reactions they engender there can arise a virulent anti-Americanism that lends strength to pacifism and neutralism and weakens the psychological-political bases of the Atlantic Alliance.

Another example of the misperceptions that exist between Europeans and Americans is the European reproach, which I often hear, that Americans, due to inadequate historical and political knowledge of Europe, do not differentiate sufficiently between totalitarian communism and democratic socialism, and that it is particularly the latter that is so attractive to Central Americans. On the other hand, I must unfortunately conclude that young Europeans, lacking an appropriate knowledge of history since 1917, consider dogmatic Marxist revolutionaries to be democrats, and, by contrast, see Americans as sinister imperialists who are insensitive to the peoples of Central America.

In his book, *Del Buen Salvaje al Buen Revolucionaria*, the Venezuelan Carlos Rangel Guevara accurately describes how many in Europe even today fall victim to the legend of the "noble savage," except that they now apply this image to the revolutionary, who is seen in a romantic light.[9] They contrast the "realm of light" of revolution to the "realm of darkness of U.S. imperialism," the sole purported aim of which is to liquidate the Sandinista regime in Nicaragua and to completely reestablish the hegemony it formerly held over Central America.

Judicious simplifications are necessary in politics in order to make things clearer to millions of people who are unable to grasp the multilayered complexities of political problems and yet who want to know from those in charge "what it's all about." But let us

---

[9] *Del Buen Salvaje al Buen Revolucionaria: mitos y realidades de América Latina*, Barcelona: Monte Avila Editores, 1976.

beware, both in Europe and America, of the *terribles simplificateurs*, especially when they presume to judge others. In an alliance that is so vital to the world, to pose as a self-righteous judge does not help; rather to act as an understanding friend, who shares the same problems, does. The journalistic principle, "bad news is good news," must not be allowed to lead to a state of affairs where European television viewers, radio listeners, and newspaper readers learn a great deal about problematical elements of U.S. policy in Central America but little about Reagan's offer to:

— support any agreement among Central American countries for the withdrawal of all foreign military advisers and troops under fully verifiable conditions and on the basis of reciprocity;

— help opposition groups to join in the political process in all countries so as to encourage competition with ballots instead of bullets;

— support verifiable and reciprocal agreements among the Central American states on the renunciation of support for insurgents in neighboring territories;

— help Central America to end its costly arms race and support a verifiable and reciprocal treaty preventing the import of offensive weapons.

I find this comprehensive offer, combined with the assurance that the United States has no intention of sending troops to Central America, to be right. But it should be constantly reiterated so that it can be understood and acknowledged by those in Europe who, until now, have nurtured their prejudices against the United States on the basis of incorrect or incomplete information. Elections and negotiations, peace and political participation, are profoundly democratic concepts that we must not allow to be stolen from us by communist sympathizers.

Some Concluding Thoughts

It is the characteristic of case studies that they always analyze very specific situations whose basic elements are unique, so their validity, when applied to other situations, is limited. This is true of Central America, which is marked by so many indigenous factors that it just reminds us of the diffused nature of the concept "Third World."

Within Central America there are not even enough common factors for one to be able to define the overall "right strategy" with which the countries of the region could achieve democracy. The case of Central America is therefore not well suited to establishing general rules of conduct regarding revolutionary change and political instability in the Third World, as the rules and strategies would have to be different for each country. Under the conditions of a repressive family dictatorship in Nicaragua, revolution was probably necessary; in any case it was no longer avoidable. But, on the other hand, supporting revolutionary overthrow in Costa Rica would be irresponsible. In El Salvador, a chance to effect change through reform arose and thus took the wind out of the sails of revolution.

Central America does serve, however, as a case study for the problems in perception between Europe and the United States. This region is as sensitive to the United States as the Middle East is to Europe. Therefore, severe strains in the NATO Alliance can arise out of misperceptions regarding Central America. There is certainly a risk that the issue of Central America could burden NATO's political cohesion to the detriment of both the United States and Europe.

Policymakers on both sides of the Atlantic are looking at this squarely. They recognize their common interest in finding a solution to the problem, and they are in close consultation with each other. The Reagan Administration's positive reaction to the San José conference indicates that the United States perceives the European stance as constructive and helpful.

According to the dictionary, "conservative" in the Anglo-American sense means: "Cautious in behavior; against abrupt changes; prefers evolutionary reforms to revolutionary violence with risky results." In this sense we Christian Democrats in the Federal Republic of Germany are also conservative in regard to Central America.

I wish to thank a number of experts on Latin America, particularly Hilde-gard Stausberg and Horst Kullak-Ublick, who gave me their useful advice and help in preparing this paper.

Daniel Oduber

A Central American Perspective on European and American Roles in the Region

For most of the post-World War II period Europeans considered Central America as merely a zone of influence for the United States. But in the last year two major events have taken place that demonstrate how important the region has become in West European eyes since the late 1970s.

On April 10, 1984, three major political organizations based in Europe and representing a large number of democratic political parties worldwide issued a joint statement on the Central American crisis. In their communiqué, Willy Brandt, Andrés Zaldívar and Giovanni Malogodi, presidents, respectively, of the Socialist International, the Christian Democratic International, and the Liberal International, expressed their concern about the increasing involvement of outside powers in Central America and urged that the social and economic strife in the region be kept separate from the East-West confrontation. Later in the year, on September 28 and 29, the foreign ministers of the ten European Economic Community nations, plus Spain and Portugal, met in San José, Costa Rica with the foreign ministers of Guatemala, Honduras, El Salvador, Nicaragua, Costa Rica and the four Contadora nations—Colombia, Panama, Mexico and Venezuela—to discuss the best way for Europe to help put an end to the conflicts in Central America (see appendix).

Both the presidents of the international political organizations in their statement and the foreign ministers in their communiqué agreed that, instead of using force, the only way to solve the problems in Central America would be to base policy decisions on two apparent convictions. The first is that the economic and social problems of the area are the true causes of the conflicts. The second conviction is that the political upheaval in these countries—

especially in El Salvador, Guatemala and Nicaragua—is essentially the result of an endless struggle between popular majorities that are being exploited and persecuted, and small groups that are allied most of the time with the armed forces and with international interests.

The Growth of European Influence in Central America

After World War II and the victory of the Allied forces in Europe and the Pacific, the United States was left on its own in Central America and the Caribbean. European powers withdrew from the area granting independence to most of their colonial possessions in the Caribbean. A series of new countries became independent members of the United Nations.

Latin American countries as a whole had been allies of the United States and of European democracies in their fight against nazism and fascism, and a large majority of Latin democratic leaders believed in the the United Nations' human rights principles. They supposed that the victorious democracies were going to become their permanent allies in the struggle against despotism and exploitation. It was this enthusiasm that led many serious political leaders in Latin America to begin their fight against dictators, and vigorous democratic leaders undertook an intense crusade to establish democracy in each of the Central American countries.

The West European countries were not in a position to worry about the problems of Latin America—least of all Central America. It was an area where the United States had the major influence and responsibility, and it was impossible to pretend in 1945 that any one of the European democracies was going to spend its time and resources helping democrats in Central America. In the years immediately following there were no discrepancies between American foreign policy and European points of view vis-à-vis the region. The reconstruction of Europe and the building of a "new world order" took all the time of the major democratic powers in the world.

By tradition and culture many political leaders in Latin America had been influenced by European political philosophies, although they had no close or formal relationships with European leaders. Also many parties in South America like the radical and socialist parties had been formed in the nineteenth century and were inspired by European thought.

In the postwar period a new wave of Christian Democratic figures appeared in Europe, like Robert Schuman of France, Alcide De Gasperi of Italy and Konrad Adenauer of the Federal Republic of Germany. They became major leaders in their own countries and, inspired by them, their South American Christian Democratic counterparts began to emerge. Socialist leaders became stronger in Latin America due to the influence of the Labour Party of Great Britain, the Social Democratic parties of the F.R.G. and the Scandanavian countries, and numerous exiled political leaders from Portugal and Spain. People like Haya de la Torre in Peru, José Figueres in Costa Rica, Rómulo Betancourt in Venezuela, and others initiated contacts with West European parties and leaders in the same way as they had already done with U.S. statesmen. The influence of European political thought was of great importance in the development of Latin American political parties of that period because the permanence and ideological structure of the European parties was closer to Latin American political behavior than was the U.S. party structure. On the other hand, newly-developed, permanent relationships with able politicians from the United States gave Latin political leaders courage to continue their fight for democracy and justice.

Many meetings took place both in Europe and America during the postwar period, and starting in the 1950s Latin American parties and leaders became internationalized in their outlook, but always with the major objective of establishing modern democracies in each Latin American nation. Contacts with the United States developed, but Europeans had a special impact. Milton Eisenhower, who during this period served as Special Ambassador to Latin America for his brother, President Dwight D. Eisenhower, was one of the first major political observers to understand the need for this change in Latin America. And near the end of the Eisenhower Administration recommendations made to the U.S. government by Presidents Juscelino Kubitschek of Brazil and Alfonso Llerás Camargo of Colombia resulted in the initiation of policies and the development of institutions to help Latin America. Yet each of the European political leaders who visited Latin America at this time had a still clearer view of the need for change and freedom in the region, possibly because they were less involved in the intricacies of hemispheric affairs.

Role of International Communism in the Region

International communism has been present in each of our countries since the 1920s. It suffered a great political setback as a result of the Hitler-Stalin Pact of 1939 but slowly recovered during the last years of the war. Nevertheless, a considerable number of young political leaders joined communist parties in Latin America out of desperation, since Latins faced a rigid and mistaken U.S. foreign policy. When finally in the 1950s democrats in the region joined forces to fight dictators, the communists of the area decided to back dictators, as was demonstrated in the cases of Fulgencio Batista in Cuba and Anastasio Somoza Debayle in Nicaragua. Even Rafael Trujillo had a good relationship with the communists in the Dominican Republic—as was usual in most Latin American countries. The split between the United States and the Soviet Union had little to do with the communist strategy of favoring dictators in Latin American countries.

For European democratic leaders, communist parties have been a fact of political life during the last decades. In Latin American democracies, on the other hand, communist parties have always been seen as a minor problem, and their electoral strength has been minimal. Communist groups have become strong in Latin America only when they have led a revolt against a dictatorship and when U.S. policy has been held responsible for the political situation. But when a dictatorship is changed into a democracy, communist forces can exist and even annoy, although they never become a major political factor in the new democracy.

Most European democratic leaders do not panic when confronted with the existence of a viable communist party; rather, they sensibly try to overcome it by encouraging other political parties to adhere firmly to democratic principles. If we study the actual political process in Latin America, we must conclude that where democracy works—as in Costa Rica, Colombia, Venezuela, Mexico, and now also Argentina, the Dominican Republic, Jamaica and other nations—the electoral strength of communist parties is small and tends to disintegrate and split into different ideological groups. Therefore, to Europeans and most Latin Americans, the only way to fight communism is through economic and social change and by the incorporation and serious participation of democratic forces in political parties, trade unions, student organizations, cooperatives, peasant leagues, etc.

In 1959 Batista was overthrown in Cuba and a group of idealistic revolutionaries came to power. Communist groups in Cuba had been allied with the dictator until shortly before his defeat. The successful revolutionaries deeply resented U.S. policy toward Cuba, and condemned the United States for the military, financial and political support it had traditionally provided to the dictatorship. It is my clear conviction that U.S. foreign policy was misguided in those days and that this alienated Cuba, thus driving it toward the Soviet sphere. Similar mistakes have been made by the U.S.S.R.—for example, in Africa, where countries formerly allied to the Soviet Union have broken their ties with the Soviets and moved closer to the Western world.

Diverging European and American Attitudes

The European attitude or view in these cases has been extremely cautious: Europeans work with a long-term vision that can assimilate changes in the world order, and they try to preserve as many friends and ideological kinfolk as possible in the Western world. Latin Americans therefore feel that European foreign policies are consistent, no matter what government is in power in a country at a given time. On the other hand, they believe that U.S. foreign policy is inconsistent and changes with each administration, often in a dramatic way.

The foreign policy of the Carter Administration was different from that of the Nixon-Ford era, and policy vis-à-vis Central and Latin America at the beginning of the Reagan Administration was totally different from Carter's. It may be that parliamentary democracies, such as those in Europe, are more accustomed to change and therefore can articulate a consistent foreign policy and assimilate internal political change, while presidential democracies unfortunately do not take into account tradition and thought in foreign policy definitions, but only their countries' transitory circumstances.

Europe's prolonged withdrawal from Latin America, and especially from the Caribbean, was essentially completed by the early 1960s—about the same time that the Soviet Union was invited into the area by Cuba. Since then American foreign policy in the region has been shaped to a great degree with the Soviet threat in mind. In the late 1960s and early 1970s, when their economies had more fully recovered, Europeans began to show interest in Latin America again, seeing the area as a possible region for investment and trade. It seemed to Latin Americans that Europeans moved into the region politically in order to expand exports and invest capital. Often the Europeans were in clear competition with the United States, but at least at the outset they were partners most of the time with North Americans in multinational ventures.

European political organizations also moved into different Latin American countries. The Christian Democrats won elections in Venezuela with Rafael Caldera in 1969 and in Chile with Eduardo Frei in 1964. The Socialist International moved in decisively to incorporate populist parties in various countries, and the Liberals have similiarly begun to organize their parties during the last few years.

All of this activity was bound to cause a reaction in the United States where many politicians and especially government officials feared the activities of the three internationals in the area. The European view of Cuba, for instance, was in permanent disagreement with that of the United States. This is not to say that the Europeans liked the presence of a Soviet-based government in the Caribbean, but rather that they did not believe that it represented a security threat to the United States.

When the Central American revolution began, the Europeans were strongly behind it and in disagreement with the United States, which they felt lacked a consistent foreign policy for helping partisans and democratic leaders fight for democracy and freedom. The retarded U.S. reaction led to a growing breach in relations with its allies. Secretary of State Alexander Haig's statements in the early days of the Reagan Administration placing Central America squarely in the East-West confrontation was a major point of disagreement between Europe and the United States.

All the European parties and governments believed (as did many Americans) that the Central American crisis was the direct result of exploitation and tyranny, and they tried as much as possible to help promote democracy and justice in the region. Even the Catholic Church concurred with this assessment and placed the Central American conflicts in the North-South context. However, it is also true that, as a result of the many failures of U.S. foreign policy, a group of countries antagonistic to the United States tried to use the revolution in Central America as a means to attack both American interests and foreign policy.

Those who supposed that the major problem of the world at the beginning of 1981 was the Salvadoran guerrillas or the Sandinista government showed an absolute lack of understanding of the real situation in this region and this resulted in undermining potential European support for U.S. policy in the area. The conflicts there, which began in 1978, have involved the killing of nearly 200,000 Central Americans; the destruction of the Central American Common Market; the uprooting of more than one million people to other cities and countries, including the United States; and the introduction of Soviet interests into a region where formerly they were unimportant. This situation was seen clearly by the Europeans (and by many U.S. citizens), and it now constitutes a major area of contention among some members of the North Atlantic Treaty Organization.

But it cannot be said that the difficulties this situation has created significantly weaken the alliance between the United States and Europe. Yet for Latin America, European efforts to solve the problems in the area are of the utmost importance. As has been pointed out, in order to establish democratic regimes that work honestly toward the development of modern societies, Latin America needs help and assistance from all democratic countries, and especially from those that are highly developed.

Regional Organizations vs. Extraregional Powers

One of the major problems of the Hemisphere is the deterioration of inter-American institutions as they were envisioned at the end of the Second World War. The transformation of the Pan American Union into the Organization of American States (OAS) and the creation of the Río Treaty took place in a world in which only 60 nations formed the United Nations. The idea was to avoid the interference of any extraregional power in the affairs of the American states. Twenty votes out of 60 in the United Nations made Latin America a significant factor in all major decisions that were important to the United States, the major superpower at that time.

Now that the United Nations has 160 members, Latin America no longer represents a "bloc" and each country gives priority to its own foreign policy rather than to regional considerations when determining its vote. The whole structure of Pan-Americanism was based on self-determination (as opposed to interventionism) and the peaceful resolution of conflict among states. The Rio Treaty considered an attack on any one of its members as an attack on all of them. The Malvinas War, the Central American conflicts, and the invasion of Grenada (to mention only recent events) clearly show that the OAS and its institutional foundations have lost relevance. The efforts of the new OAS leadership raise the possibility of revamping the whole system, but such an endeavor will take time and will require the support of all members. Conflicting interests now inherent in the foreign policies of major Latin American countries, however, make an agreement with their big partner, the United States, very difficult.

When it is said that the OAS sought to keep out the non-regional powers, it is meant that Europeans were excluded from the major political decisions of the Hemisphere. First, there was the threat of Nazi Germany and later, that of Soviet Russia. However, Soviet presence in the Hemisphere is a reality today, and the greatest challenge to hemispheric leadership is how to meet the threat it brings. Some statesmen feel that the only solution is a military one, but the majority feel that there are other solutions. In this respect there are considerable differences of opinion between U.S. officials on the one hand and European and Latin American statesmen on the other.

Role of the United States

As I have mentioned, most of Latin America feels that the Central American conflicts are caused basically by economic and social realities that were ignored by American foreign policymakers for many decades because they were interested only in protecting U.S.

investments, no matter what kinds of government were in power in the region. Private business determined American foreign policy in Central America, the Caribbean, and throughout the entire Hemisphere.

Certain attempts were made to change this: the Good Neighbor Policy, the Alliance for Progress, and later, the Caribbean Basin Initiative, but on the whole, U.S. embassies were only concerned about the investments of U.S. corporations. The result has been catastrophic in terms of hemispheric relations, and, because information was available to larger segments of the Latin American population, a much greater resentment accumulated against the U.S. policy of ignoring dictatorships, assassination, torture and exploitation.

In order not to fall into the hands of Soviet communism, which continually tempted the Latin American intelligentsia, most Latin leaders turned to free Europe—to its political parties and its international organizations—for moral support for their struggles. In the 1970s Europe returned to Latin America, and European political ideas and experience helped foster change in the Hemisphere, specifically in Central America and the Caribbean.

Mexico, Venezuela and Colombia, the major countries in this area, also became more involved in the struggle against dictatorships and injustice. The Catholic Church became a major partner in this cause, and slowly an important alliance was forged among all democratic political parties in the area with the aim of establishing democracy and justice in this part of the Hemisphere.

The United States did not act. Its permanent hesitation vis-à-vis this movement made it appear to be an ally of the "status quo." American investments were well protected by dictators, and whenever a reformer appeared he was immediately characterized as anti-U.S. and then as a communist. Dozens of democratic leaders were branded as communists due to a permanent misunderstanding on the part of U.S. officials who listened only to the characterizations made by members of privileged groups, both native and foreign. European leaders began to be aware of this situation and became friends and supporters of these Latin American leaders, in many cases saving them from becoming communist pawns out of frustration.

The turmoil of the last few years and the failure of the Organization of American States forced Latin Americans to act independently of the United Sates in working out the problems of Central America and to exclude the solutions—mostly military—proposed by U.S. officials. The major countries of the region (Mexico, Venezuela and Colombia), together with Panama made the unprecedented decision of regrouping as a team to begin the tedious and difficult task of pacifying Central America.

The Contadora Process and Washington

These four states formed the Contadora Group, named for the Panamanian island where they first met in January 1983. The Contadora initiative has patiently advanced despite great obstacles and the reluctance of many officials in the United States to accept a Latin American solution to Central America's problems. Contadora now has the backing of the United Nations, the Catholic Church, all Christian groups in the area, all Latin American countries, most European and Asian democracies, as well as the People's Republic of China and communist countries in Europe. Contadora recommendations are strongly supported in the United Nations. Yet there is a bitter feeling lingering for Latin Americans and Europeans because there is no strong support for Contadora from the United States government.

There are, of course, limits to serious differences between the United States and Europe over the problems in Central America, but many in the region feel that U.S. allies in Europe, Asia and Latin America are certainly astonished at the overreaction of U.S. policy with respect to the Central American conflict. The spheres of influence of the past are now being questioned. As mentioned above, each European and Asian friend of the United States takes into consideration many other problems when formulating foreign policy; Latin America is no exception. The solid bloc of the postwar period is now finished: the Malvinas War was proof of that.

This does not mean that, in the event of a major conflict between the United States and another superpower, its Latin American friends would not join efforts with the United States. It means, rather, that only in such a situation would it be possible to reestablish a tight alliance. With regard to other problems such as trade, external debt, migration, investments, marketing, etc., it is impossible to assume that Latin American nations will place U.S. interests above the national interests of individual Latin countries. The example of Argentina selling its wheat to the Soviet Union in spite of the Carter boycott clearly showed the supremacy of national interest. Similarly, the participation of the United States in the Malvinas War is an example of the United States putting its interests above international treaties.

The major disagreement between the United States and its European and Latin American allies centers around the security issue. For the current U.S. Administration, the problem of Cuba and its role in Central America and the Caribbean can only be solved by strong military action. In an incidental way the United States is trying to help the small Central American and Caribbean countries by means of the Caribbean Basin Initiative and similar programs. With all its military might, the United States does not really have to worry about security. Rather, it should seek to acquire neighbors as reliable as Canada by helping the countries of Central America and the Caribbean develop economically and socially. Terms of trade, external debt, migration policies, scholarships, technology transfers, and investment policies that respect each country's characteristics and institutions, will do more for stability and peace than any military solution—which inevitably leaves resentment, instability and continual struggle.

For this reason the first chapter of *The Report of the National Bipartisan Commission on Central America*, which outlines a number of goals for the region, including rapid progress on the political, economic and social fronts, was very well received, while the military and security recommendations were not. Both Europe and Asia can participate in the kind of program outlined by the Commission, and we are sure that no problem will arise that could create tensions between the United States and its developed allies with respect to non-security recommendations. But a program of this kind needs multilateral participation, as was clearly expressed by the 12 European foreign ministers when they met in San José.

We can forsee a peaceful Central America only when problems over differences in ideologies are not interpreted as security issues. Introducing Central America to the negotiating table of the superpowers was a mistake made by the United States. Such a purely regional problem could have been solved with the help of Latin

American countries acting within the Hemisphere. Now, whether we wish it or not, we have been sent to the conference table of the superpowers, and this makes solutions more difficult. Let us hope that the Contadora countries, together with the rest of Latin America and Europe, can find solutions in these next years. This will enable this issue to be withdrawn from the East-West confrontation and to be placed where it belongs: in the North-South perspective. We are sure that within this context the United States and its friends on all continents can work together.

Appendix

Joint Communiqué of the Ministerial Meeting of San José, Costa Rica

1. A conference of Foreign Ministers was held in the city of San José, Costa Rica on 28/29 September 1984 between the European Community and its member States, Portugal and Spain, the States of Central America and the Contadora States.

2. The Conference was attended by:

For the European Community

H.E. Mr. Peter Barry, T.D. *Minister of Foreign Affairs of Ireland, President of the Council;* H.E. Mr. Giulio Andreotti *Minister of Foreign Affairs of Italy;* H.E. Mr. Robert Goebbels *State Secretary, Ministry of Foreign Affairs of Luxembourg;* H.E. Mr. Hans van den Broek *Minister of Foreign Affairs of the Netherlands;* H.E. Sir Geoffrey Howe, QC MP *Secretary of State for Foreign and Commonwealth Affairs of the United Kingdom of Great Britain and Northern Ireland;* H.E. Mr. Léo Tindemans *Minister of External Relations of Belgium;* H.E. Mr. Uffe Ellemann-Jensen *Minister of Foreign Affairs of Denmark;* H.E. Mr. Hans-Dietrich Genscher *Minister of Foreign Affairs of the Federal Republic of Germany;* H.E. Mr. Yannis Haralambopoulos *Minister of Foreign Affairs of Greece;* H.E. Mr. Claude Cheysson *Minister of External Relations of France;* H.E. Mr. Edgard Pisani *Member of the Commission of the European Communities*

For Portugal

H.E. Mr. Jaime Gama *Minister of External Relations*

For Spain

H.E. Mr. Fernando Morán López *Minister of Foreign Affairs*

For Central America

H.E. Mr. Fernando Andrade Díaz-Durán *Minister of External Relations of Guatemala;* H.E. Mr. Jorge E. Tenorio *Minister of External Relations of El Salvador;* H.E. Mr. Edgardo Paz Barnica *Minister of External Relations of*

149

Honduras; H.E. Mr. Miguel D'Escoto Brockman *Minister of the Exterior of Nicaragua;* H.E. Mr. Carlos José Gutiérrez Gutiérrez *Minister of External Relations and Religion of Costa Rica*

For the Contadora Group

H.E. Mr. Augusto Ramírez Ocampo *Minister of External Relations of Colombia;* H.E. Mr. Bernardo Sepúlveda Amor *State Secretary of External Relations of Mexico;* H.E. Mr. Oyden Ortega Durán *Minister of External Relations of Panama;* H.E. Mr. Isidro Morales Paúl *Minister of External Relations of Venezuela*

Observer for the Permanent Secretariat of the Secretariat of the General Treaty for the Economic Integration of Central America

Mr. Rodolfo Trejos Donaldson

3. Inspired by a consciousness of their shared cultural heritage and of their common attachment to the ideals and values enshrined in the United Nations Charter, the participating countries have inaugurated through this conference a new structure of political and economic dialogue between Europe and Central America. They are convinced that this dialogue, and the increased practical cooperation that it will engender, will reinforce the efforts of the countries of Central America themselves, with the support of the Contadora States, to bring an end to violence and instability in Central America and to promote social justice, economic development and respect for human rights and democratic liberties in that region.

4. A comprehensive discussion took place between the Ministers of the Ten Member States of the European Community and those of the Central American countries on the political, economic and cultural relations between them and agreements were reached on the future development of those relations. They have agreed that further meetings in this dialogue should take place at regular intervals. The level of such meetings, whether at ministerial or official level, will be determined in the light of circumstances. The Foreign Ministers of Spain and Portugal associated themselves with these agreements.

5. The Foreign Ministers exchanged views on current regional and international problems and developments, and in particular the situation in Central America. They expressed their preoccupation at the conditions and acts which gravely disturb the peace and security of the Central American region, and agreed on the necessity for the Governments of the

area to intensify negotiations which lead to mutual understanding and permanent stability.

6. The Ministers reaffirmed their commitment to the objectives of peace, democracy, security and economic and social development, and political stability in Central America and were united in the view that the problems of that region cannot be solved by armed force, but only by political solutions springing from the region itself. In this conviction they affirmed their support for the pacification measures which are being developed in the Contadora process. They expressed their conviction that this process represents a genuinely regional initiative and the best opportunity to achieve a solution to the crisis through political undertakings aimed at the achievement of the aims set out in the "Document of Objectives" approved by all the Governments of the region on 9 September 1983. They noted with satisfaction the progress achieved so far towards such a solution, and that the revised draft Contadora Act for Peace and Cooperation in Central America is a fundamental stage in the negotiating process for the attainment of peace in the region. They called on the States concerned to continue to make every effort to bring the Contadora process rapidly to final fruition through the signature of a comprehensive agreement which would bring peace to the region. They were agreed on the necessity for a practical commitment to the implementation of any such agreement by all the States in the region and all other countries which have interests there, and on the necessity for the verification and control of that implementation.

7. The European countries expressed their willingness to support, within their capabilities and if requested, the efforts of those states to which it falls to implement the provisions of any agreement.

8. The Ministers discussed the international economic situation and, in particular, economic and trade relations and cooperation between the European Community and Central America.

9. The Ministers agreed that the current international economic situation should be regarded as particularly difficult. In this context, they underlined the problems concerning the external indebtedness of the developing countries and the wider economic, trade and social implications of continued indebtedness for those countries. Within this framework, the Central American Ministers stressed that in present circumstances debt servicing by the countries of Central America is even more burdensome given increased interest rates and deteriorating prices for those products

which make up the bulk of their exports. The Community Ministers and those of Portugal and Spain declared themselves ready to assist the countries of Central America, in the appropriate framework, in the pursuit of policies aimed at solving these problems.

10. The Ministers expressed their determination to cooperate in the appropriate international fora with a view to improving the present international economic situation.

11. An effective manner of contributing to the reduction of political tension in Central America would be to support the actions intended to preserve the degree of economic interdependence existing between the countries of the region.

The Community Ministers recognized that the Central American region has a definte development potential through the process of integration and reaffirmed their willingness to support this through the further development of relations between the two regions.

In this connection, the Ministers looked forward to the accession of Portugal and Spain to the European Community and welcomed the contribution which they will make to the further strengthening of cooperation between the two regions.

12. The European Ministers and those of the Central American isthmus declared themselves satisfied with the results already produced by their relations and agreed on the need to broaden and deepen these relations. They concentrated more particularly on the areas in which cooperation with the European Community has proved useful for the economic development of the group of Central American countries and where mutual cooperation should be strengthened (specific development projects, particularly agricultural and rural projects with a regional basis, regional integration, trade promotion and generalized preferences).

13. The European and Central American Ministers, in looking ahead to the future, in the perspective of the development of mutual cooperation, recognized the existence of solid ground for cooperation activities, on the basis of equity, respect and mutual benefit, notably along the lines of the following paragraphs.

14. The Community and Portugal and Spain and the group of Central American countries recognized the need to develop, extend and diversify their mutual trade to the fullest possible extent. In this connection the Ministers considered that the generalized system of preferences could be

an appropriate means to encourage the growth of foreign trade and industrialization of the countries concerned. They agreed that the use of the system should be simplified and its benefits be extended.

The Community reaffirmed the importance it attaches to the fundamental objectives of the generalized preferences system and announced its intention, where the development and the application of the system is concerned, of taking into account the interest that will be shown by the Central American countries.

15. Taking account of the importance of economic development for the countries of the Central American region, the Community will do everything possible, within the context of its present and future programmes in support of developing countries, towards the development of the region. These actions should be identified by common agreement, based on the priorities and objectives of the region and should be multilateral in character. The Community declared itself willing to exploit to the full the institutional infrastructure existing in the region.

In addition to aid given on a bilateral basis by Member States of the Community to the countries of the region, the Community will provide technical and financial assistance to Central America, in particular for agricultural, agro-industrial and rural projects. With the aim of promoting regional economic integration and the development of intra-regional trade, it is the intention of the Community to give priority assistance to projects of a regional nature and to help the countries of Central America and their regional institutions through sharing with them the Community's specific experience acquired in matters of integration.

For its part, the group of Central American countries declared itself ready to present specific projects in priority fields, which take into account inter alia social welfare aspects.

By way of illustration, mention was made, with regard to projects, of the demands which were presented jointly by the countries of Central America to the international financial community in Brussels in September 1983.

The Central American Ministers emphasised the importance they attach to the reactivation of production and particularly of the production of goods traded within the Central American isthmus. For the purpose of the latter, financial support is required for the countries of the Central American isthmus, preferably through the Banco Centro-americano de Integracion Economica (CABEI), so that that support will contribute to the reactivation of the industrial and agricultural sectors of the region.

It is the intention of the Community and of its Member States to give priority to the development of their assistance to regionally-oriented projects and to those of a social nature such as health programmes and those intended to relieve the situation of those who for one reason or another have been compelled to abandon their traditional homes.

16. The Ministers on the two sides considered that economic cooperation represented an area of interest for future relations between the Community and the group of Central American countries. In this context, they mentioned specifically the promotion of business contacts between the two regional groupings, cooperation between public and private national financing instruments in the two regions, as well as scientific, technical and basic training, especially in research fields. The Community Ministers took note of the possibility offered by the CABEI Board of Governors to open its membership to countries outside the region.

In view of the important role assumed by foreign investments in the economic development of Central American countries, the Ministers agreed that the promotion and protection of European investments in Central America are in their mutual interest. In this connection, they stressed the need for an improved climate for investments in the region by appropriate measures of encouraging private investments.

17. The Ministers of the European Community and those of Central America acknowledged the interest in strengthening and giving institutional form to their mutual relations. Acknowledging the importance of strengthening relations, they declared themselves ready to start discussions as soon as possible with a view to negotiating an inter-regional framework cooperation agreement. On the Community side, the agreement would be negotiated in accordance with its established procedures. Both sides considered that the conclusion of an agreement of this type would confirm the political will of both regions to extend and develop their relations and that it would also help to reinforce relations between the Community and Latin America as a whole.

18. The Central American Ministers expressed the view that the appropriate intergovernmental forum for approving the main lines of a regional position as a mechanism for negotiation and follow-up in the economic sphere is the Central American Economic Council, with the participation of a representative from the Government of Panama.

The negotiating body, under the aegis of the Central American Economic Council, will be an ad hoc group composed of delegates from every Government. This body will act in coordination with the group of Heads of Mission of the countries of the Central American isthmus (GRUCA), with headquarters in Brussels. The SIECA will support the mechanism for negotiation and follow-up and will seek the collaboration of other institutions connected with Central American integration and other regional and international bodies in accordance with the circumstances.

19. The Ministers expressed their conviction that this meeting constitutes a first step in a process which will effectively increase existing cooperation between Central America and Europe.

20. The Ministers participating in the Conference of San Jose paid tribute to the President of the Republic of Costa Rica on whose initiative the Conference was held. They expressed their profound gratitude to the Government and People of Costa Rica for the warm welcome and generous hospitality which has been extended to them and their delegations and voiced their appreciation of the courteous and efficient organisation of the Conference.

21. The Minister for External Relations of Costa Rica thanked the European party warmly for their expressions of gratitude, and on behalf of the five Central American states thanked the European Community and the Ministers of its Member States, the Ministers of Portugal and Spain and the Ministers of the Contadora Group of States for coming to Central America and for their significant contribution to and constructive work at the conference, all of which factors would determine its success.

Recent Publications of the
Council on Foreign Relations

A Changing Israel, Peter Grose, Vintage Books/Random House, 1985.

Prospects for Peace in the Middle East: The View from Israel, Presentations made at a conference held in cooperation with The Dayan Center for Middle Eastern and African Studies, Tel Aviv University, Council on Foreign Relations, 1985.

Strategic Stalemate: Nuclear Weapons and Arms Control in American Politics, Michael Krepon, St. Martin's Press, 1984.

North Africa: Regional Tensions and Strategic Concerns, Richard B. Parker, Praeger Publishers, 1984.

Soviet Policy in Eastern Europe, Sarah Meiklejohn Terry, editor, Yale University Press, 1984.

The Making of America's Soviet Policy, Joseph S. Nye, Jr., editor, Yale University Press, 1984.

The Dilemma of Reform in the Soviet Union, Timothy J. Colton, Council on Foreign Relations, 1984.

Unemployment and Growth in the Western Economies, Andrew J. Pierre, editor, Council on Foreign Relations, 1984.

The Russians and Reagan, Strobe Talbott, Vintage Books/Random House, 1984.

Nuclear Weapons in Europe, Andrew J. Pierre, editor, Council on Foreign Relations, 1984.

For complete catalog and ordering information please contact Publications Office, Council on Foreign Relations, 58 East 68th Street, New York, N.Y., 10021. (212) 734–0400.